HAVE YOU SEEN MY
Brother?

*Discovering That God Is Good
Even in a Tragedy*

MARGIE CRETELLA

ISBN 979-8-89130-256-3 (paperback)
ISBN 979-8-89130-257-0 (digital)

Copyright © 2024 by Margie Cretella

All rights reserved. No part of this publication may be reproduced, distributed, or transmitted in any form or by any means, including photocopying, recording, or other electronic or mechanical methods without the prior written permission of the publisher. For permission requests, solicit the publisher via the address below.

Christian Faith Publishing
832 Park Avenue
Meadville, PA 16335
www.christianfaithpublishing.com

Printed in the United States of America

DEDICATION

I would like to dedicate this book to my brother Father Steve. Thank you for letting me spend the last ten years of your life with me and letting me now share it with everyone else. You have taught me the true meaning of faith and the goodness of God. You have a true belief in your Creator, and you never question the answers that he gives you to your prayers even though they might not be the answers that you are looking for. Ralph Waldo Emerson said, "It's not the destination. It's the journey." If he could meet you now, I'm sure that he would say to you that you are on an inconceivable journey. Continue your journey with the Lord, Father Steve, and it will take you to more places than only he can imagine for you!

Father Steve celebrating Easter Mass
at Liberty Healthcare Center.

CONTENTS

Acknowledgments .... vii–viii
Introduction .... ix–x
A Letter to My Brother 1–3
The Car Crash 4–10
Is God Really Good? 11–13

Medical
St. Elizabeth Hospital 14–18
Cleveland MetroHealth Hospital /
MetroHealth Old Brooklyn Medical Center 19–31
Baclofen Pump Surgery 32–33
The Emergency Room 34–38

Heartwarming Stories
A Box of Chocolates 39–42
Appalachia Mission Ministry 43–45
Hurricane Katrina 46–48
Pope Francis 49–51
Shoes 52–56
The Blue Light Special 57–59
The Garden of Hope 60–65
Water 66–68
Who's the Real Angel Here? 69–73

Faith to Friends
Faith to Friends 74–75
Faith 76–77
Family 78–83
Fishing 84–86

Food 87–89
Football 90–91
Friends 92–94

Father Steve's Family
Father Steve 95–102
Father Steve and His Siblings 103–104
Charlie 105–110
Margie 111–119
John 120–123
Elizabeth 124–127
Father George 128–130

Father Steve's Favorite Things
Heaven's Angels 131–132
Prison Ministry 133–134
Thanksgiving 135–136
The Chosen 137–138
Travel 139–141
Walking with Braces 142–145
Wall of Memories 146–152
Weightlifting 153–156

Father Steve's Favorite Children's Books
Beans, Beans, and More Beans 157–158
Death and Dying 159–160
Father Steve's Favorite Blue Engine 161–163
Not One, Not Two, but Three Trees 164–165
The Invisible Connection 166–168

Father Steve's Favorite Adult Books 169–171
Father Steve's Favorite Songs 172–173
Life in the Nursing Care Facility 174–185
Reminiscing with My Brother 186–189
The Road of Life 190–195
Yes, God Really Is Good! 196–201

Epilogue 203–208

ACKNOWLEDGMENTS

To my husband, Mike, who constantly exceeds expectations by respecting our marriage vows when it comes to "in good times and bad." You have never given up on Father Steve or me no matter how far we push you. You have embraced many bad times in the last ten years, and you do all that you possibly can do to turn my bad and trying days into better and happier days. You have the patience of Job, like in the Bible, and you handle my brother's ministry with the utmost respect. You take great care of my brother and me, making sure that all our needs are met. This is living proof that it pays to marry your best friend.

To my son Mikey, who was the first to review this book, and who had to honestly tell me if he thought that I had anything worthy of what he felt could even be called a book. Thank you for helping me to turn my title into a book that I truly believe in. I never thought that I could be worthy of writing a book about Father Steve, but you helped to raise my confidence, getting me to this point. Thank you for taking so much time and energy to proofread and edit my book, thus helping me to present my thoughts to the readers. Your dedication as a son was exemplified by your ever patient and unconditional love and support. I couldn't have done it without you!

To my sons Tony and Joey, and my daughters-in-law Risa, Stefanie, and Rachel for your continued love, support, and encouragement throughout the last ten years. All of you help me get through the tough and scary times that encompass my life. You listen to my stories, watch me cry and cheer me up. All of you make sure that my five grandchildren (Vincent, Isabella, Caleb, Gianna, and Alaina) are always ready to be there for me and to put a smile on my face. By sharing your children with me, I can reach a level of true happiness!

To my siblings, Charlie, Elizabeth, and John. Thank you for all sticking together on this ten-year journey. It's been a different journey for all of us because of the distance between us, but we all have the same goal in mind and that is to make the best decisions for Father Steve. We all want him to be healthy in mind, body, and soul. We also want him to be challenged, productive, safe and at peace. He survived the last ten years, so I believe he reached these goals. We will continue to always help him to keep those once made goals in mind.

A special thank-you to all the healthcare workers who have provided wonderful care for Father Steve throughout the years and who have always respected his ministry. Thank you to Windsor House for the constant over-the-top care for my brother. Thanks to our friends and family for continually checking on all of us for the past ten years. Your cards, messages, phone calls, food, and gifts have been appreciated beyond what you can imagine. May God bless all of you!

To a charming little café and market named Good Intentions, located on State Route 87 in Kinsman, Ohio. Whether I sat by the window watching it snow, or sat by the fireplace, it was a place where I did a lot of my writing for this book, ate some wonderful meals, and enjoyed a latte or a mimosa. Their mission statement is, "To have every person that comes through our doors leave healthy, loved, and inspired to be the good in the world." It is a place you truly might want to visit.

INTRODUCTION

My brother Father Stephen Popovich, also known to many as Father Steve, is a unique, quirky, generous, entertaining, good-hearted, tenacious, and devout Catholic priest. On November 13, 2013, while working, he met up with an unexpected and unimaginable freak accident that placed him on an unbelievable journey. With a lot of prayer and determination, he fought against all odds of what could possibly go wrong in almost ten years. While on this journey, God would challenge his faith far beyond what he could have ever imagined. Father Steve will show you how he exhibits an immeasurable amount of faith in his life. His story will make a lasting impression on your life and in your heart. He says, "I will always keep the faith and win this race." His faith is endless and admirable.

The accident left him paralyzed from the chest down, but his heart, mind, and soul were salvaged, leading him to an amazing life of faith-filled experiences. He taught me how to find God in the worst of times.

His family is on his journey with him. At times, his siblings feel like they are on an upside-down roller coaster at an amusement park. At other times, they feel as though they are on a merry-go-round going around in endless circles and never being able to get off. Occasionally, the merry-go-round slows down. They think there might be a chance for all of them to get off, but it picks up speed again. Maybe it's giving them more time to find their true meaning of our good God in their lives. They all find out that they need the good God just as much as their brother does.

I learned more about God in these last ten years than I had my whole life, and my short stories will help you to see how I found a loving God who really was, and has been, with my family this whole time. I wasted so much time looking for him in all the wrong places.

Would our lives be filled with sadness, struggles, and disappointments, or would a happy ending come our way? Read on to find out where we all stand and if Father Steve is literally standing with us.

Hopefully these short stories will make you smile and inspire you to also find the true goodness of God like I did. Don't make the mistake of looking in all the wrong places. He's right there next to you. Happy reading!

Father Steve and his sister Margie.

A LETTER TO MY BROTHER

Father Steve,

I'm not quite sure if you will ever choose to read this book. You're very humble, and I know that you don't like to be the center of attention, but you did give me the okay to write.

I can envision the book on your tray table next to your bed or wheelchair. It may end up in your lap one day, or you may even embrace it from time to time. It may be just too hard for you to use your fingers to turn the pages of the book and relive the last ten years of your life. It might be a bit much for you to find out so many things that happened to you that you can't recall because you were too sick. The accident and medical part may be a little too hard for you to digest. I understand that, and it's all okay.

Please read on, Father Steve. Skip the medical pages if you choose, and read on to see the brighter and faith-filled days and memories that we all share with you. Revisit the years of your life, and see how your difficult moments and days have turned into beautiful little memories and miracles.

This book was simply written to tell a story about a Catholic priest who put God first in his life despite a tragedy that struck his own life. It's a story about how you used your faith to teach everyone that God is good every day in everything. Your life shows how you never even lose that glimmer of hope, faith, and trust that God will show up. I see how the healing power of prayer to God now works right in front of my very own eyes.

You taught me the importance of keeping God first in my life and not ever questioning his decisions, as hard as they may be. I know that faith is believing in the unknown and accepting God's plan. After spending so much time with you, I now understand this. I have had many teachers in my life from kindergarten to college, but none have made an impact on my life like you have.

There is a saying that goes, "The most beautiful thing to see is a person smiling, and even more beautiful is to know that you are behind it." I hope that if you do read this book, Father Steve, I will make you smile!

I'm not only proud to say that I know you, but much prouder to say that I am your sister and had the opportunity to write about you and share your story. I have learned from you the true meaning of determination, and how volumes of prayer and unquantifiable faith can make little miracles occur. Thank you for teaching me the true importance of a faith-filled life. Mom and Dad would be so very proud of you as I am.

You truly are one of my best friends, and I love and respect you more than life itself.

Peace and God bless,
Margie

Damaged chalice from car crash.

THE CAR CRASH

For I know well the plans I have in mind for you—
oracle of the Lord—plans for your welfare and not
for woe, so as to give you a future of hope.
—Jeremiah 29:11 (NABRE)

The dreaded phone call! The one you never want to get. There's never a good time for it, especially if you're on vacation and 650 miles from home.

Most Wednesdays were typical for this priest from New Middletown, Ohio, but this Wednesday would be different. He had no idea that when he walked out of the door of the rectory, he would never return to the home that he so much loved. Routinely, he would celebrate Mass at his parish, St. Paul's, and would then make his way to the Ohio Maximum Security Prison to celebrate Mass with the prisoners. But November 13, 2013, wasn't a typical Wednesday at all because with a twist of fate, he never made it to the prison.

Morning Mass went as usual, and Father Steve gathered up some of his birthday presents from the morning women's group who attended Mass. They were anxious to send him off with some cake and gifts for his upcoming birthday on November 24.

He was ready to go and fulfill his priestly duties, making sure that the trunk was packed first. The trunk of his car contained what he considered precious cargo! It was his prison ministry bag, which contained everything that he would need to say his morning Mass at the prison. It contained his Mass prayer book, chalice, ciborium, a hand towel, purificator, altar cloth, wine and water cruets, wine and hosts, a crucifix, and his stole that he would wear. He was good to go! Or so he thought.

It was a silent morning because when black ice takes over like a thief in the night, you are sliding in silence with no means of slowing down, let alone stopping. There was no screeching of tires.

The black ice put the small white Grand Am on a scary and gruesome path that would alter the life of its occupant, Father Steve. The black ice spun his car around, sent it crashing into a truck, not stopping until the car landed on a stranger's property and smashed into their tree. I still wonder if he even saw the truck coming toward him. What could he have even felt to see that his car was headed for a tree, and he had no means of stopping it? How scary would that be, especially when you are all alone? How could black ice, something so transparent, be so deadly? Where on earth was God?

To one living in northeast Ohio, this wasn't an unexpected scene after a freezing night of rain. On the night before the accident, our weather forecaster warned us that the morning would come with some roads being covered in black ice. My husband texted Father Steve the night before, warning him about the slick morning that was ahead of him. Nothing on earth could have warned him about the morning that he was about to experience and how it would change his life forever.

After smashing into the tree, the only thing he barely remembered was a police officer climbing through his back window to check on and comfort him. He was in and out of consciousness. The fire department, along with the ambulance, arrived next. To this day, we don't know who made the 911 call. I wish we did so that we could thank them.

Now was the time for the police department to make that dreaded phone call. Who would make it, and what would they say? They barely had any information on Father Steve's condition except that he was alive. His wallet was found, and the search began for the emergency number to be located. Fortunately, he was organized, and the number of my husband Mike was found. Unfortunately, we were far away in Goose Creek, South Carolina, visiting our son Tony and his wife, Stefanie. Our next stop was to travel to Savannah, Georgia, to visit our son Joe and his fiancé, Rachel. Joe and Rachel would be getting married the following July, and we were going there to help with their wedding plans. Their marriage was to be officiated by Father Steve.

Mike was conversing with Tony, and I just sat down to read a book titled *You'll Get Through This*, by Max Lucado. A few weeks earlier, my brother Father Steve, gave me this book to read. He often shared one of his "good reads" with me. I couldn't figure out why on earth he would give me a book like this. My life was perfect. My marriage was beautiful; my children and my whole family were safe and sound. All our jobs were going well, and life was grand! I decided to read it anyway in case my life was ever turned upside down, so I took it on vacation with me. Little could I have imagined what was in store for my family. Did my brother somehow have a premonition about what was coming shortly in his life?

I opened the book and began reading the first page. I read Max Lucado's words,

> You'll get through this. It won't be painless. It won't be quick. But God will use this mess for good. In the meantime, don't be foolish or naive. But don't despair either. With God's help you will get through this.

As I finished the last word of this quote, the phone rang. It was the call that would change the lives of my family forever. I guess this was Max's warning to me. Oh my gosh, does he know my brother and God's plan for him? Max Lucado tells us that God often uses messes for good. I so hoped that the phone call wouldn't be about a mess that someone was in. It ended up being much more than a mess. It was a disaster!

The phone rang, and Mike informed the police department that the wallet belonged to his brother-in-law. Mike was his emergency contact person. The police department had very little information for us. They explained that there was a car crash and that my brother was in and out of consciousness. Yes, he was alive, and that seemed to be the best news we could get. He was rushed to St. Elizabeth's hospital in downtown Youngstown, Ohio, where he was put into the ICU with no movement in his legs, and uncontrollable flailing arms. Word got out quickly, and some clergy members and close friends were at the hospital before he even arrived.

The five words that came out of my mouth were, "I want to go home." I immediately started praying. My son, Tony, immediately got on the phone to book us a flight home and said that he would drive our car home later and then fly back to South Carolina. It would have been too stressful and exhausting for us, plus unsafe to make the twelve-hour drive home. Suddenly, the word *home* just sounded so very far away. I immediately called my sister Elizabeth, who lives and works in Cleveland, and I told her that I didn't know much but that she needed to get to Father Steve at St. Elizabeth's hospital in downtown Youngstown.

Now it was time to call everyone and anyone that we thought could find out some information for us. After sending a family member to the hospital to check on Father Steve, he told us that things didn't seem to look very good, and the word *paralysis* was being used. Now it was time to call Elizabeth back and forewarn her that she might be walking into a bad and sad situation. I quickly called and let her know the news that I had and that we'd be on a flight home as soon as possible.

I called my brother Charlie, who was working in Ashland, Ohio, and then called my brother John, who lives and works in California. With not much to report, I felt bad because I left them hanging. They arrived within a day or two. The clergy was called next, and I found out that a priest was already there with him. Relatives and friends were now notified and told to spread the word and please start a prayer chain because now was the time we truly needed God's help. Where was God anyway, and why did this even happen? How could the word *paralysis* be thrown around now? My brother needs those legs to stand behind his altar. Did God forget my brother was a priest and that he needs his hands to celebrate Mass? How would he fold his hands in prayer again or give a simple blessing? Maybe this is just a big mix-up. Lots and lots of questions flooded my mind ever so quickly.

I immediately began bargaining with God. I needed to figure out what my bargaining chip would look like because this kind of bargaining was not like the bargaining I would do at a neighborhood garage sale. I put my best bargaining face on, and I was ready to go! I had to figure out how to negotiate with a higher-up, let alone the most important being that I would come against—my Creator!

After searching for hours and trying to figure out what I could offer God for what he could do for me, I realized that God is not a yard sale, and he is not to be bargained with. We shouldn't try to manipulate the Lord, and I needed to stop that immediately. I am reminded of a quote from Shannon L. Alder, an inspirational author and therapist. She tells us, "Bargaining with God is pointless. He already has a thousand followers that will do what you bargained to do for free." How would and could I bargain with God against people who would do what God asks of them for free? Who was I that I wanted something in return? I now needed to take my bargaining chip and throw it away for good. Mahatma Gandhi tells us that a man of faith does not bargain or stipulate with God. I guess God probably didn't want and could do without that extra $20 that I would put in the Sunday collection anyway.

It was now time to face reality. It was a very scary time, but time to suck it all up and do what we needed to do to get back home. My husband and I packed up just enough of our things to fit in one suitcase for the plane ride home, and my son would bring the rest of our things home later. Our flight wouldn't arrive till almost 11:00 p.m., so we had a long day ahead of us.

Our phones rang constantly all day long from people who heard about the news and wanted answers from us even though we had none. Talk about feeling helpless and scared. It must have been the same feelings that were going on inside my brother's head. Luckily, my sister was there the whole day until we got there around midnight. I can't imagine what was going on in her head staring at him and being prepared to make decisions about his care. She said that the whole time, he would pound his leg with his fist trying to see if he could feel his legs. His arms were flailing around because the spinal cord was also trying to figure out what was going on and how much damage had occurred. Was any or all of this going to be fixable?

The day seemed like forever, but luckily, my son, Tony, and daughter-in-law, Stefanie, were with us. They were great company for us and kept us busy until it was time to take us to the Charleston airport and say goodbye. The plane ride seemed so very long and exhausting. So many emotions were going on in my head. I would look around the plane and wonder if anybody else was going home to a mess like we were. Most of the passengers looked happy and content, apparently coming home from a vacation down South. I still searched for a person who looked like they may be headed for an awful situation like me. I wanted to reach out to them to comfort them, but I also was looking for someone to comfort my husband,

and myself. A total stranger would even do. I kept thinking about my brother lying there and not being able to move and probably so scared. How could he possibly be paralyzed, he still had so much to do? His ministry was far from complete. How would he hold his prayer book or Bible again? My scary world was beginning to crumble, but I needed to stay focused until I got home to see exactly what the situation was.

When we arrived at the airport in Canton, my daughter-in-law's family picked us up and were able to take us to our home. We quickly dropped off our suitcases, ran out the door and drove to St. Elizabeth's Hospital.

IS GOD REALLY GOOD?

> Taste and see that the Lord is good; blessed is the stalwart one who takes refuge in him.
> —Psalm 34:9 (NABRE)

"God is great, God is good, let us thank him for our food. By his hands, we are fed. Give us Lord our daily bread. Amen." This is a popular meal blessing that many of us learned at a very young age.

My brother has taken three words from this short prayer and turned them into his daily mantra. "God is good" is a popular phrase Father Steve uses several times a day. He often starts his day this way before his first cup of coffee and daily newspaper, and these may be the last few words he mumbles before he falls asleep at night. He often begins and ends our conversations this way too. He will repeat this mantra as he greets family, friends, doctors, nurses, waitresses at his favorite restaurants, and even strangers.

Father Steve was always adamant when he would look me in the eye and simply say "God is good." I always agreed with him no matter the day or time of day. Recently as we sat enjoying breakfast at his favorite spot, he called out to me, "Hey, Marge." Immediately I set my fork down, grabbed a knife, and eyed the jelly selection. Would he want grape jelly, strawberry jelly, or apple butter on his toast? When I questioned him to see if jelly was what he wanted, he very simply replied, "No." And yes, you guessed it, he once again looked at me and just said, "God is good."

Every time my brother said these three words to me, my mind wandered to many places. Technically, yes, God is and has been good to me and has blessed me abundantly, but I still have lots of questions about him.

How can my brother always insist that his Creator is so good when his life has just been turned upside down? If God is really that good, where was he when my brother's car slid aimlessly on black ice, hitting a truck and slamming into a huge tree at the entrance of some stranger's driveway? Why was he left paralyzed from the chest down, remaining in the same condition 3,454 days later? Why does he continuously let Father Steve get transported by ambulance to the hospital with repeated infections that often leave him in a septic state? According to the doctors, he has been close to death a few times. How would we get through all this? I constantly asked, "Where is our God, and why was God a 'no show' so many times in almost ten years?" So many unanswered questions at one time is so overwhelming. I wondered if all, or even any of my questions would ever get answered.

I was raised in a strict Catholic home. Our days at home were very busy and fun-filled, and they had a religious vibe to them. I was very close to my parents and siblings and knew that we were all protected by God. We never missed Mass on Sunday, and we attended a Catholic grade school and Catholic high school. We even had our house blessed every year by the pastor of our church, which was called "chalking the door." The year and initials of the three kings who visited Jesus at his birth were inscribed above the door. We were good to go. Nothing could possibly go wrong in our lives.

Besides going to Mass, I pray the rosary often, and I go to the Stations of the Cross during Lent. I have been a Eucharistic minister for thirty-plus years, distributing the body and blood of Christ to my fellow parishioners, family, and friends. I taught Bible school in the summer for many years and even volunteered at our church festival to raise money for the parish. I was the director and prekindergarten teacher at a Catholic school where I may have been the first person to introduce little innocent five-year-olds to the wonders and world of Jesus. I donate to various organizations, and I help at our church food pantry. I feel that I lead the ultimate Catholic life. My uncle Father George Popovich was a priest, and my brother aspired to follow in his footsteps, which he did. I believe that my family had an advantage when it came to God taking care of us. I envisioned very little chaos coming our way, and it appeared that we were all set. We weren't good; we were golden!

Much to my dismay, my golden world did come crashing down on my family, and it would change our lives with a new normal that I didn't feel I could ever accept.

Our journey now begins! We will spend the next ten years learning the fate of my brother and how God plays his role in our lives throughout these years.

ST. ELIZABETH HOSPITAL

> Trust in the Lord with all your heart, on your own intelligence do not rely: In all your ways be mindful of him, and he will make straight your paths.
> —Proverbs 3:5–6 (NABRE)

Father Steve was rushed to St. Elizabeth's Hospital in downtown Youngstown, where he was immediately put in the ICU. St. Elizabeth's Hospital is a large brown building with a white cross placed on a solid brown wall. It was a hospital frequented by me for many years to visit sick friends and family along the way. I gave birth to my three boys at this hospital, so I had great memories of it too. I had a sick feeling in my stomach though as we approached this building that this would not end up being a great memory to add to my list.

Mike dropped me off at the door as he parked the car. I ran in and quickly demanded the room number to where my brother rested quietly in bed. I already panicked, worrying that I wouldn't be able to find him. I remembered asking many people where my brother was. Never could I have imagined back then and throughout the next ten years that I would still be searching for my brother, let alone write this book titled *Have You Seen My Brother?* and have such a journey ahead of us. Now I really needed God for many reasons. If he couldn't show up tonight, then I expected him to come with the morning light.

Not being sure of what I would find and how I would react, I prayed hard and with tearful eyes tried to come up with the right words to say to him. What if I said the wrong thing? What if the look on my face made him realize the extent of his injuries. I took a couple deep breaths, walked into the room, and made eye contact with my teary-eyed sister. The look on her face didn't promise me a lot of hope, so I cautiously walked toward his bed. My sister Elizabeth had been at his side all day, until Mike and I made it home from South Carolina. As I approached his bed, he looked at me and said, "And you thought that if I did have an accident, I would have been on my motorcycle." And yes, I did, because we had that conversation previously so many times. I had a fear of his motorcycle and what it could do to him. I knew he was a cautious driver, but what about the other drivers on the road?

Father Steve needed his rest, so our visit was short. Mike stayed that night, and we decided that he would take the midnight shift; I would take the day shift. We would then meet in my brother's room daily, relay any medical information that we had, and send each other off with a kiss and hug. My sister spent that night with me, and we woke up to a beautiful sunrise. Was this God's way of letting me know that everything would be alright? I almost couldn't wait to go to the hospital to see if my brother would be sitting up in bed. Well, much to my dismay, nothing had changed, and I almost didn't recognize the man in the bed. What happened to that beautiful sunrise that gave me confidence that I would walk into a brighter situation? Why didn't God have time for us?

When we arrived at the hospital, we were met by a lot of discussion about spinal cord injuries and possible surgery. We tried to keep my brother calm, and he very much appreciated our constant companionship. A very special visitor, the bishop of the Youngstown Diocese, Bishop George Murry even stopped in for a blessing, prayer, and a visit. He was very much welcomed by Father Steve.

The man who invented the stretch bands to exercise with even heard about my brother's accident and came to see if he could be of any assistance. He literally stood on a chair, jumped into the air, and landed in a split on the floor showing how flexible he was. He asked us if we would like to be able to do the same thing. My brother John and I sat there, with puzzled looks on our faces, knowing that wouldn't be an activity we would plan on doing in the future. Father Steve was amused by him and appreciated the fact that he was interested in trying to help him. The people that we would meet on this journey will be remembered by us forever. Friends came to simply pray with my brother and sit by his side in silent company.

The number of visitors became so overwhelming at the hospital that the head of the ICU department was called in, and visitors were limited to only clergy and family. If you weren't on the visitor list, you couldn't get in. People would call and beg me to be put on the list. One of my brother's closest friends told me he was about to go out and buy a black shirt and obtain a white collar to pass as a clergy member but felt too guilty impersonating a priest, so he decided against it. It was heartbreaking to tell his friends that they couldn't come to visit and pray. I made many visits to the hospital chapel looking for some guidance and peace.

It was decided that Father Steve needed surgery soon, so the doctor on call came in and explained a little bit about the upcoming surgery, which was scheduled for the next day. We all waited with much anticipation for the next day in hopes of a positive outcome.

The surgery seemed like an eternity. A prayer group from the parish where Father Steve was stationed at, St. Paul's, came and offered their prayers as a group and invited us to join in. The word of the accident spread very quickly throughout the community and parishes, and I can't imagine how many people were praying at that very moment. There was no way God wouldn't show up now, and I was confident that he would stop whatever he was doing because so many prayers were coming his way at one time for one person. All I prayed for was that he would make it through the surgery. They say prayers can move mountains. Well, move over, Mount Fuji, Mount Kilimanjaro, and Mount Everest! Our prayers will knock you over!

Our prayers were answered, and the doctor came out to let us know that Father Steve was alive and that he had made it through the surgery. The doctor told us about all the limitations that he would have and pretty much explained to us that he would not be able to walk again. He touched his thumb to his index finger and said that he did not have the expertise to do what was needed to be done for my brother to be able to do that simple task. He said that you need to be able to touch your thumb to your index finger to turn a key, grasp a small object, or hold on to things. At the time, I really didn't care because all I wanted for him was to be alive. I never thought or imagined that one day in the future it would be difficult for him to raise a host and chalice again at Mass to represent the body and blood of Christ.

When the doctor told us that probably there was not a chance of him ever being able to walk again, I realized at that moment that I had forgotten about his lifeless legs, and my concern only was that he would live. I needed to get God back on the radar again. Oh gosh, did he already leave the hospital, and where might he have gone? So many other people were praying for so many other things at that time he could be anywhere. I then thought about how I reverently prayed and asked for his life and nothing more, so there, as simple as can be, he answered my prayers just as I requested. I needed to be grateful now. I'll catch him on another day to work on the legs. Father Steve made it through the surgery by the grace of God and a miracle.

It was now time to leave the hospital and go to the towing yard to remove any articles from my brother's car. We emptied out the glove box and then ventured to the trunk. The trunk was already opened from the car crash, and we removed the prison ministry bag that he used for Mass at the prison. We opened the bag there and sadly found his once-perfect chalice and ciborium collapsed. My eyes became teary-eyed because somehow, I had hoped that they would be perfectly intact. The hosts were scattered in the bag, and some were smashed. We disposed of them properly even though they had not been consecrated yet.

The following two weeks were very intense. My brother acquired a bedsore on his sacrum from lying still in bed. This would become an issue later, but keeping him alive was way more important now. Father Steve had his days and nights confused and literally stayed up for three days straight at one point. He stared straight at the ceiling and never made any eye contact with any of us.

I think it was at that very moment that I would look at him and wonder who this man was lying in bed? I even checked outside the door to make sure that I had the right room number. I began to get very nervous and scared, almost not recognizing the man in the bed and almost demanding that I wanted them to find the brother that I left behind before my trip to South Carolina. What did they do with the brother that I had known for fifty-eight years? I wanted him back, and I wanted him back right now! The man lying pretty much lifeless in this bed was not my brother. Where was he, and what had they done with him? I was not happy and almost wanted to go and search through the hospital looking for him. Thus, the title of this book was already written in my head, *Have You Seen My Brother?*

My brother was a big guy with the frame of a body builder. Everyone who knew him said that they would hear him before they even saw him. He was loud and loved by all because of his generous heart and wallet. His outgoing personality helped him to make friends who were loyal to him and him to them. He had a great rapport with everyone, and being a Catholic priest, he was able to take care of his parish and, often, people in the outlying community. He showed them how to live a faith-filled life. He was there from the beginning of people's lives, often baptizing them as children. He took care of them spiritually throughout their lives while they received the sacraments of the Catholic faith. He also was there often up to the very end of people's lives too as he gave them a final blessing and performed the anointing of the sick. He was and is a humble priest who puts God first in his life.

So that was the brother that I wanted back. I wanted the loud, fun-loving priest who loved the spontaneity of the day. He loved a welcomed adventure and a great challenge, and he loved a good dare. Wow, I can't believe I just wrote those words because maybe this car crash would be his big adventure, challenge, or dare in his life. Would God dare him to get through the years that were ahead of him, and would God promise to hold his hand to get him through it? I should have learned by now that all adventures, challenges, or dares aren't meant to be fun. Some dares turn out to be disastrous. I had no idea a challenge, adventure, or dare in his life would and could come to this—let alone, why God would let it!

CLEVELAND METROHEALTH HOSPITAL
MetroHealth Old Brooklyn Medical Center

Have no anxiety at all, but in everything, by prayer and petition, with thanksgiving, make your requests known to God. Then the peace of God that surpasses all understanding will guard your hearts and minds in Christ Jesus.
—Philippians 4:6–7 (NABRE)

It was now time to find a place where Father Steve could receive some intense spinal cord therapy. Since my sister lives in Cleveland, she was able to talk to several doctors that she was friends with about spinal cord patients and what facilities offer excellent care and therapy for these patients. The facility that was named was MetroHealth Old Brooklyn Medical Center, and there was an opening. We needed to move quickly. Father Steve was moved shortly after the decision was made and began his journey on December 13, 2013, in Cleveland, Ohio, that would last until March 17, 2015.

He was admitted and was known as a C7 spinal cord patient. Within a few days after he became a patient, he complained of neck pain.

He was quickly moved to Cleveland MetroHealth hospital, a few miles away. This facility was a very tall building covered in glass panels with a bluish-gray tint. The MH intertwined aqua and blue logo rest on the top of the front of the building. On either side of the main building are two large circular buildings that are attached. It looked so huge making me wonder how many patients it could possibly house. Would my brother get lost in this huge place, and would I get lost looking for him? Once again, I would begin the search for my brother. You almost needed a map once you got in there to find your way around.

They moved quickly with him, and an X-ray was immediately taken to see what was causing the pain. Much to their surprise, a screw had become loose from the first surgery, so another surgery was scheduled quickly. The spinal cord doctor who performed the surgery said that he would surgically enter through the front of his neck first. If Father Steve was able to withstand the surgery, they would then turn him over and enter through the back of his neck to continue to fix the problem. The surgery took hours, but during the surgery, they came out to tell us that he was doing well and that they would be able to turn him over to continue. More hours continued, and the doctor finally came out to tell us that everything went well. With this surgery, my brother's neck was more stable, and now he would be able to touch his thumb to his finger.

Very shortly after the surgery, it was time for the halo brace to be put on to keep Father Steve's neck and spine moving as one with his body so that the spinal injury could heal. My husband and I were told that we could leave the room for the procedure if we had queasy stomachs. We volunteered to stay to support my brother, but little did we know what the procedure entailed. Once the door was shut, we felt pretty much committed. The ring around his head was held in place with four screws or pins. The ring was then attached by four bars to a stiff, lightweight vest that fit around his chest. Several shots were inserted into his skull to help to numb the area. If he said that he felt any pain, the area was shot up again. I've never seen such long needles. The screws were literally screwed into his skull as we watched. One side was done and now it was time for the next side of his skull to be done. *Okay, God, anytime that you would want to step in here, you would truly be welcomed.* I thought that by now I had pretty much seen everything, and now I knew I had seen enough. It is now ten years later, and he still has scars from the procedure.

He needed to wear the halo brace all the time to allow for the neck surgery to heal and for his neck to be stabilized. It looked unbelievably uncomfortable. The neck brace was tight around his neck, and it was hard for him to talk, let alone understand him when he talked. He got very frustrated at times. His stay at Cleveland Metro was very short because it was important to get him some intense physical and occupational therapy as soon as possible.

Father Steve's next move was back to where he started from, a wonderful rehabilitation center called MetroHealth Old Brooklyn Medical Center. Old Brooklyn, as it was called, was an older brown brick building. It had the same aqua and blue MH logo outside with a big arrow pointing to Metro Health Rehabilitation Institute of Ohio. This building would be his home for a year and a half except for when he had to go back to the main hospital for surgery.

He was soon introduced to the motorized wheelchair and what would become his legs. It was very hard the first time that I saw him in the wheelchair. My eyes teared up, and I remembered turning my head away so that he wouldn't see me. I didn't know if I would have the strength to suck it up and put a cheery smile on my face. I then looked at him and wondered, *What did this rehab place do with my brother—the full of life, strong, rock of a person brother?* This person in the wheelchair did not resemble him at all. If he could have just stayed big and loud, I wouldn't have always felt like I was in this same predicament. It was never hard to keep track of him before. Why was everybody losing my brother?

He loved his Superman and Batman shirts. He always wanted to wear them, so somewhere in my head, I was almost convinced that he had the power of either one of these characters. It was foolish and childish on my part, but it seemed to make me feel better. I figured that it would be okay though, because he would probably only be in the wheelchair for a short time until he would get stronger, get feeling back in his legs, and get those shoes back on his feet to walk out of that building. I made sure that his shoes followed him whenever he was moved from hospital to rehab because I felt that deep down inside, those shoes would find a place on the ground, not the foot plates of a wheelchair. There was no way that I felt God, who was referred as the Divine Physician by the early Church Fathers, could possibly let him require a wheelchair for the rest of his life. He had a lot more, literally, running around to do; and we still had a lot more polka dancing to do. And what about his ministry? How could he continue that?

He needed to spend time learning how to use this wheelchair and be able to maneuver around the hospital. I can't count how many times this wheelchair and any future wheelchair would run over my feet and his phone. He had to be able to lift himself and move around in the wheelchair to eliminate any future sores. He already had one that needed to be dealt with shortly.

Old Brooklyn was an absolutely wonderful hospital. My husband and I drove back and forth daily from Youngstown to Cleveland, ate out of vending machines and the hospital cafeteria. We eventually expanded our food palate to some local take out. Many friends gave us gas gift cards since we were traveling daily to the hospital. It was great to stop, get gas, pick up coffee, a quick snack, and be on our way either going to or coming home from the hospital. Thank you to all these people!

My sister Elizabeth lived and worked in Cleveland, so she was a very big help. She was able to come to the hospital many times to visit and bring in whatever food that our brother was craving that day. She literally ran all around town picking up his desired take out. My sister and I spent a lot of time together discussing our brother's future while trying to make reasonable plans for him. It took a lot of teamwork and discussions to make sure that we were making the correct choices about his future and to figure out what was best for him. We wanted to make sure we covered anything and everything that could possibly go wrong with the care that we would choose. We often had to make quick spur-of-the-moment decisions about his medical care and whoever was with him at that moment needed to realize that their choice was wise and educated and was out of love for him. His siblings would all support that person's decision.

We learned a whole lot about spinal cord injuries and watched diligently when Father Steve would do occupational and physical therapy. We wanted to be able to help him in any way that we could after he was discharged. My brother met amazing doctors and nurses who taught him all about his spinal cord, and he, in turn, taught them all about Jesus. Even if you weren't Catholic, you learned about Jesus. It was just Father Steve's thing!

It was getting close to Christmas and not a fun time for anyone to be in the hospital. My one morning began with the introduction to the mother of a seventeen-year-old girl. She approached me as I sat in the gathering section drinking a cup of coffee as I was waiting to visit my brother. I needed to wait until the doctor did his rounds to assess him, so I had time to meet this wonderful woman. This mother, who found out about our situation, sat down next to me, and asked me what we thought about God. She heard that my brother was a Catholic priest and that he was working in his ministry at the time of his accident. Her seventeen-year-old daughter had been in a sledding accident. Her daughter got hurt innocently, not drinking, not doing drugs, or anything that would harm her. All she wanted was to have fun sled riding. I immediately took her to my brother's room introduced her to him and told him that this mother wanted to know what he felt about God. I left them all alone and she stayed there for quite a while. The friendship between my brother, her daughter, and both our families flourished for months.

My brother enjoyed the company of the energetic young seventeen-year-old. She in return enjoyed the company of a Catholic priest, and they shared each other's visitors. Whoever visited my brother would go and visit her. Whoever visited her would come to visit my brother. He then had many young people visiting him, which was good because he was so young at heart. We prayed together, ate together, and laughed together. The two of them got each other through the rough and tough days. They even had wheelchair races down the hallway just for fun.

This young girl had a tutor come in to help her finish her senior year of high school. She was the bravest seventeen-year-old that I have ever met. After a few months, it was time for the young sled rider to go home. She graduated, but unfortunately only lived about another month after graduation. She passed away on July 4, 2014, and the doctor let Father Steve leave to attend her funeral service and give a little homily.

We met a few lovely Amish families while we were there too. Their injuries were usually extensive due to the nature of their jobs in construction, such as working on roofs or operating heavy machinery. In either case, there's just too much that can go wrong in their situations and occasionally does. We became close to these families. Many of their children would come to visit, and they raised the spirits at the hospital because young children have a great way of doing that. We shared our food with them, and they shared their food with us. When the Amish families would go home, I'm sure their whole community would pitch in and help with cooking and the chores that needed to be done. I found the address of one Amish family that has been in my wallet for ten years. The father was injured quite intensively. It might be time now to pull out that address and make a visit there this summer to check on them and see how they are all doing. Plus, the Amish country is a beautiful place to visit.

Wound Surgery

Within a few weeks from being admitted to Old Brooklyn, the decision was made that the wound on his sacrum needed to be addressed before any intensive therapy was started. The bigger that the wound got, the longer it would take to heal, so surgery needed to be scheduled soon. He would not be able to do intensive therapy and be constantly moved around while he had a wound that was constantly getting larger.

He needed to go back to Cleveland Metro for the surgery. After the surgery, he would be moved to a special unit in that hospital, typical to that of a nursing care facility. This special unit was considered a long-term facility for the recovery of patients such as my brother. They warned him that it would be difficult and that he probably wouldn't like it, but it was necessary. His time there was monotonous and seemed like forever. He needed weeks and weeks of lying on his back until the wound was completely healed.

A wound or pressure ulcer is an injury to the skin and underlying tissue resulting from prolonged pressure on the skin. People who are at most risk are people like Father Steve who is unable to change positions. He became educated in bed sores because he suffered from a few of them. Right after his accident, he could not be moved because of his condition, which led to a plate-sized bed sore on his tailbone. The pressure of lying on your tailbone can cause a pressure sore quickly. They start very small but seem to grow ever so fast. Treatment and recovery can last for months if the sore has progressed to the fourth stage. A wound doctor in Cleveland completed surgery on Father Steve for pressure sores on two different occasions.

The wounds are cleaned by scraping out all the dead tissue and applying special medicine. Father Steve's wounds were so severe that a wound vac was necessary. A wound vac is a vacuum assistant closure using suction pump tubing and a dressing to remove excess exudate and to promote healing. If this did not work, surgery would be mandated. Surgery was intense and often having the same area worked on was very serious. Skin must be grafted from other parts of the body. This meant that not only would the wound need to heal, but the area that the skin was grafted from had to be healed as well. The wound surgery was successful, but the doctor literally said he did not want to ever see my brother again. The surgeon said that he couldn't possibly work on the same site again. Not enough skin is left there to work with.

After the surgery, he had to lie on his back for weeks at a time. He would count the holes in the ceiling tiles. His meals were eaten while lying on his back. Imagine eating soup lying down. I would give my brother a plate of food and use it like a clock. I just would tell him the pineapple is at twelve o'clock, the cantaloupe is at three o'clock, the strawberries are at six o'clock, and the honeydew is at nine o'clock. He would then know where to put his fork and what fruit he would stab with that fork. After he ate, he would just lay on his back, mostly in prayer, listening to music and trying to sleep. They really needed a TV on that ceiling. Being short, I had to stand on a chair to converse with him. Weeks seemed like months to me—I can't imagine what they felt like to him.

After weeks of lying on his back, it was time for him to begin sitting up. The Hoyer, a portable total-body lift was used to move Father Steve from the bed to the wheelchair. The Hoyer lift consists of a huge sling-like contraption. The patient is very carefully placed onto the sling, which is hooked in place overhead, and the patient is moved ever so slowly to prevent any other complications. The medical staff would Hoyer him into his wheelchair, where he would sit only for a few minutes at a time because his blood pressure would drop very quickly. He was then Hoyered back into bed, where he would lay until the next day to repeat the procedure all over again. Every day they would increase the time that he would spend in the wheelchair to make sure that he could tolerate the changes in his blood pressure. I remember him playing polka music to make the time go faster. This process continued until the doctor felt that his blood pressure was tolerable and that his wound was healed. He also needed to be able to function and go back to the physical and occupational therapy that he needed. The whole healing process took about six weeks.

To this day, in order to prevent new wounds from forming, he needs to be constantly moved during the day. During the night, he is moved from side to side every two hours. There is no slacking from this routine, or Father Steve will be the one to pay the price of another surgery. The nurses are always on top of this routine and check his skin a few times during the day. He has been doing wonderfully, thanks to the nursing staff!

Father Steve came back to Old Brooklyn in April 2014 to begin some intense therapy. Old Brooklyn was wonderful to him. He went to physical and occupational therapy every day. It was often very exhausting, and patients helped to encourage each other to get through the sessions. We often did some of the exercises with him just for some fun competition. He had to move disks over a plastic arc. When he did this, we would mention a special person in his life and told him to try one more time just for them. More names were added to the list to give him encouragement.

There were days when he loved having a cheerleader there, and other days when you got *the look*. *The look* kindly meant, "Please be silent. I just want your presence here and not a whole lot more." We all accepted *the look* because we had no idea what he was going through and what was going on in his head and never wanted to question him. Maybe we were a little afraid of the answers that we would get. He worked with blocks a lot and had to move blocks from one side of the bin to the other side of the bin. This would help with the mobility of his hands. He would try to repeat this exercise and beat his previous time from the day before. They had Father Steve fry an egg on the stove one day, and trust me, that was very painful to watch.

During physical therapy, there was a table that he was Hoyered on to. It was called the tilt table. The medical staff would lay him down on the table and strap him down in several different places. He would be raised up a little at a time as his blood pressure was closely monitored. Each time, he was raised up only ten more degrees until he was able to get into what was considered a standing position. He would hit a balloon back and forth to us. It was so nice to see him in somewhat of a standing position.

He did many exercises to strengthen his hands and arms. He worked with some clay on the table pushing the clay back and forth as if he was kneading dough. Inside the clay was an item that he needed to try to retrieve. He also played checkers with the therapist which was great for his hand-eye coordination and finger mobility. It was also good for his mind because he had to strategize since he did not like being a loser.

He worked on a hand bicycle which was great for his hands, arms, and shoulders. He tried to improve how much time he spent on the bike every day. Resistance was added to the bike to challenge my brother's strength and mobility.

He also did a lot of exercises on the mat. He would lie down, and they would spread his legs open and closed, which they called the snowflake exercise. It almost looked like he was making a snow angel in the snow. This would help to keep his muscles from atrophying. They also had him sit up on the side of the mat. This was extremely hard for him, and the first time he was only able to sit up for about thirty seconds. Whenever he sat up on the mat, he would put on a quick motivational song or maybe something like the theme from Rocky. Every day he would try to improve that time by maybe just a few seconds.

My brother also joined in with the painting activities for a few days and painted some nice pictures that were matted and framed. My favorite one—a picture of the "Footprints in the Sand" poem—is hanging on my family room wall. Doing this painting exercise was extremely important for finger, hand, arm, and shoulder strength. He wasn't always in the mood for art activities, but I tried to encourage him. Maybe I was just being a little bit selfish because I just wanted another art activity gift from him. During that therapy, my brother was reminded of how important it was for him to continually move and try to lift himself in the wheelchair so that he would not get any pressure ulcers.

Father Steve made many friends at the facility. Doctors, nurses, other patients and their visitors all became his friends. Everybody knew that they would be there for a while, so they were all looking for comforting, friendly-faced people to rely on. Some people were in horrific accidents such as shootings. Others were there for therapy after a simple fall at home. Either way, everyone was friendly to everyone because everyone needed each other.

Father Steve's very good friend who owned a restaurant back home would bring food to him because my brother wasn't very fond of hospital food. He would either bring in food or we would pick it up on our way to the hospital. This was done many times. His very generous friend not only fed my brother, but during the Lenten season, he brought up food for the staff at the hospital and our family. Some patients would even make their way over to the amazing spread that he sent over because they knew a good meal was coming their way. Everyone looked forward to the fish on Friday. Oh, how this friend took care of him! Doctors and nurses began to learn more about Father Steve by just watching how his family and friends handled him and how they took such good care of him.

Sadly, there were several patients at the hospital who didn't have any visitors at all, and you knew who these people were because when they were in the rehab unit, they were doing exercises in their pajamas. There was no one to even bring them clothes to wear. These were the patients who would enjoy any food that they received from Father Steve's spread. My brother not only had clothes to wear but had great food to eat. He had nutritional food, and he also had a lot of munchies.

On Saturdays, my brother would celebrate Mass in the gathering room. Staff, patients, and visitors would all come and join in. Many Catholic people looked forward to this Mass because receiving Communion was important to them. Even people who weren't Catholic would attend because they knew that Father Steve would share a homily that would help to get them through the week in the tough world in which they lived in. He was able to distribute ashes on Ash Wednesday, and he had quite the turn out. We all celebrated the forty days of Lent together in the hospital.

When Father Steve was officiating Mass on Saturday at Cleveland Metro, a girl who attended the Mass had met him earlier because she was a surgeon's right-hand person. She worked with the surgeon who did hand surgery. After Mass, she told us that she felt bad that she felt as though she wasn't really paying attention to the Mass but was watching Father Steve and his hands. She felt that the surgeon could really help him with some surgery to help bend those fingers and straighten out those fingers on his left hand. The surgeon soon examined him and knew that he could help Father Steve out by making those fingers bendable to be able to grasp his chalice and be able to hold on to it better. They explained everything that they would do with the tendons on that hand, and the surgery was scheduled and was quite successful. Father Steve was in a cast for a while but was very pleased with the outcome. His Saturday Masses became easier for him, and now he didn't have the fear of dropping his chalice. God was on his side while he worked with the surgeon who very much respected the life of my brother's ministry and him being a priest.

There was a prayer service one Saturday when my brother had to stay lying down in his bed. I can't specifically remember what the issue was, but that was the position he needed to be in. He knew that he couldn't celebrate Mass, so he at least did a prayer service with the homily from his bed. I remember standing there looking at him thinking, *Who are you?* Once again, I had those thoughts in my head of *Where is my brother?* My brother shouldn't even be sitting in a wheelchair, let alone lying in a bed giving a faith-filled homily to his little gathering. He should be standing upright like he did for fifty-eight years. What is with all this sitting in a wheelchair, lying in bed, and talking about God to people who probably wondered why God had not healed him yet? Things just didn't seem right here, and they were so very hard to accept. I'd like to just go to sleep one night, wake up, and have my brother standing there in front of me in the morning, ready to go like he always used to be. I wanted him to be full of energy and vibrant in life. I search for these days in my head and hope that they won't be forgotten for good.

Soon it would be Easter, and the weather would start getting warmer. We were told that Father Steve was allowed to go outside of the hospital and drive around the perimeter of the hospital and go no further. We took advantage of the beautiful weather and my husband, Mike and I decided to go for a walk with my brother. We followed all the instructions, we walked, and my brother drove his wheelchair and went around the perimeter of the building. Like a little kid who just saw a candy store, my brother eyed Walgreens across the street and just took off, and I'm sure that he never looked both ways. He bought a pair of sunglasses, talked on his phone for a bit, and then bought handfuls and handfuls of goodies and munchies. He was very excited to see what a little bit of freedom was. I was so nervous the whole time hoping that nothing would happen to him since we were not permitted to be there. Who would I call, and what would I do if something did happen?

The trip was safe, and there were no hiccups, so I felt we didn't have to do any explaining when we got back. For some reason, we thought that no one would notice the bags of munchies that he was so excited to have. We went back to the hospital, entered the elevator, and went up to the sixth floor where his room was located. The nurses who noticed Father Steve with all the bags just turned their heads the other way. He rode up and down the hallways delivering all his goodies and munchies to all the friends that he had made. I thought it was actually a great experience for him because he realized that someday he would have the freedom to be able to get out and about. He now realized that he could go into a store, shop around, and buy whatever he wanted. He hadn't been out and about for almost four months. So to me, it was a beautiful day, not only sunny, but an eventful day for him. I think the nurses all felt the same way because no one ever questioned any of us about the Walgreens trip.

Occasionally, there were plan of care meetings about my brother with doctors, nurses, occupational therapists, physical therapists, and family members. These meetings were held to discuss his present condition, his progress, and what his future looked like to all of them. It didn't look like an easy future, but a future no less. A lot of what Father Steve did with the future would be up to him.

A small plan of care meeting with myself, my sister, my husband, and the spinal cord doctor was planned and carried out. We just assumed that Father Steve would stay there for probably two years getting therapy. The doctor looked at us and asked us, "Where will your brother go in six weeks, and who will he live with?" I looked at my husband, my husband looked at my sister, my sister looked at the doctor, and the doctor looked at me. We went around the circle various times in the same order. We had no idea what he was talking about because we thought the life of a spinal cord patient here at the hospital would be much longer than what he was presenting to us. The doctor explained that years ago, spinal cord patients usually stayed there for one year. With insurance coverage changing so much, the length of stay for a spinal cord patient changed to nine months, then six months, and eventually would just become six weeks. How could they let my brother go home in six weeks when he had so much more therapy to do and improve so much more? He truly had potential, not just because he was a new patient, but because it was my brother that the doctor was talking about. He had no idea how much determination Father Steve had and how nothing could stop him reaching any goals that he put in front of himself. We almost panicked as to what his future would be and where he would live out this future. Since my brother still had a few medical issues that needed care, his stay lasted much longer than the six weeks that were planned at the beginning. After sixteen months, the journey would begin to find a home for my brother.

BACLOFEN PUMP SURGERY

> When you call me, and come and pray
> to me, I will listen to you.
> —Jeremiah 29:12 (NABRE)

Successful surgery comes Father's Steve way by means of a baclofen pump in his abdomen. Baclofen is a very effective medication that is used to decrease the spasticity in my brother's extremities as a result of his injuries. He had a lot of spasticity in his legs, which needed a plan of treatment. Spasticity is involuntary muscle contractions that will cause stiffness and tightness. This medication, baclofen, also controls dystonia which is a muscle contraction that can result in twisted or abnormal postures. The medication is used to improve hyperactive reflexes and excessive muscle tone. This is used often for spinal cord injuries. The baclofen pump is an intrathecal delivery system. The medication goes right to the appropriate site in the spinal cord. Without the baclofen pump, Father Steve would have his legs falling off the footrest because he could not only feel his legs or feet, but muscle contractions would take over. The muscle contractions were often jerky and would be bothersome, but not painful because of his paralysis.

Before the surgery could be performed, baclofen pump assessments were performed by a physical or occupational therapist. A small dose of baclofen is inserted into the spinal cord, and the patient is assessed to see what the effects of the medication can do. My brother was curled up in the bed before the injection was placed in his spinal cord. I looked at him and said to myself, "Oh my goodness, who are you? You are not the big guy that I remember. Where is my brother who could bench-press four hundred pounds?" He looked so small in the hospital bed. If the test was successful, his surgery would be performed with a short hospital stay. A small dose was injected into his spinal cord.

We called upon God once again and prayed because we wanted this procedure to work. God once again listened as we called upon him, and in a few hours, my brother's legs had totally straightened out. It was a success, and the surgery date was marked on the calendar. Father Steve looked forward to the surgery to help control the annoying spasms.

The surgery date arrived, and the baclofen pump catheter was implanted under the skin and in his abdomen. The pump contains a battery that lasts between five and seven years. Father Steve has already had it replaced. The pump is programmed to meet with a small computer, and a wand is placed over it which communicates with the pump. One end of the catheter is inserted into the pump and the other is inserted into his spine at different levels. The surgery was successful and so needed by my brother.

After the surgery, the surgeon talked to us and commented that he thought I had a quirky brother. Well, I totally agreed with him. He said he would love to just sit and have a cup of coffee with him someday. I thought to myself, *Yes, a quirky guy, and his favorite cup of coffee—you never know where that conversation would go.* I'm sure it would go to a wonderful place like where all his conversations go just like his homilies. Putting a pot of coffee in front of him is like putting the pulpit at church in front of him. You'd leave his company with a witty and funny story. The conversation would end with some great advice, just like his homilies do. It would be a cup of coffee and a time that you would never forget!

THE EMERGENCY ROOM

> Be sincere of heart and steadfast, and do not
> be impetuous in time of adversity.
> —Ben Sira 2:2 (NABRE)

Ten years of doctor visits, hospital stays, and ER visits made up a good part of my brother's last ten years. They have made Father Steve who he is today. It's an important part of his journey. My brother has spent a lot of time in the last ten years in the ER room.

The phone call informing us that my brother would be taken to the hospital by ambulance was usually never expected. He was taken to St. Elizabeth hospital, where he got very good care at each one of his visits. We were pleased with the attentiveness and respect given to Father Steve. Most of the time, he was too sick to care or too confused by the sepsis setting in due to a UTI that he didn't even remember the ambulance ride. I'd get the call, meet him at the hospital, and hoped that we would get to leave and not be admitted. That part seemed to never happen.

It's always cold in the ER room because hospitals can combat bacterial and virus growth with cold temperatures. All your senses are stimulated when you go to the ER and sit in the bay. The bay is a room with a curtain as its door. I guess you have to consider yourself lucky that you got into a bay, and you didn't have to lie in the hallway. The first sense that is aroused is a sense of smell. That antibacterial or bleach smell lingers in the air. All you smell are antiseptic and cleaning products. Your sense of sight is enhanced by everything that is so sterile and bright-looking it's almost as though it's as bright as a spotlight. The sharps container of used contaminated syringes, needles, scalpels, and lancets hang on the wall right next to the laundry basket for dirty hospital gowns and dirty blankets. A chair sits right under the sharps container and next to the laundry basket. You'll see a computer screen sitting on a high table, and there usually is a TV in the room. It's never a quiet place in the ER. Your sense of hearing perks up quickly. Carts are pushed up and down the hallway, and you hear everything because there are no doors, only curtains. People are moaning and groaning in the bays and in the hallways. Some are calling out for the doctor, but most are calling out for God. Some are faint cries, and some are shrieking loud screams.

Then there is the sense of touch. I'm a bit of a germaphobe, so I tried not to touch anything in the room. When my brother needed comfort, I held his hand. That was needed for him and me because I never knew if he'd make it through that visit, and it might be the last time that I would get to hold it. I would stare at the only chair in the room, but since it was sitting under the sharps container right next to the laundry basket full of dirty clothes, it kept me in an upright position. You'll rarely experience the sense of taste there because eating is usually not permitted. Most patients are not permitted to eat while testing is being done in case surgery may be required. No visitor should possibly be bold enough to eat in front of these patients. I would only have a cup of coffee if my brother had fallen asleep.

During some of these visits, my brother would spend time just staring at the ceiling and never blinking or making any eye contact with anyone. It's a very scary environment that I've envisioned too many times. When he stares at the ceiling and doesn't make any eye contact, I always become very afraid because I don't know if I'll get him back and wonder what I would do if he didn't know me. How do I deal with someone who doesn't even recognize my face? I now get that uneasy feeling like I can't find my brother again. This person lying here and not making eye contact with me certainly isn't the brother of my past.

The trip to the ER usually ends up in hours of anticipation waiting for X-ray results, blood test results, CAT scans and so on. The last ER visit had the nurses jabbing four individual sites before his IV site was deemed successful. My brother's arms are very sensitive because the paralysis has left him with most of his feelings in his arms. I've seen him go through some surgeries easier than when they poke for the IV or port sites. Some of his veins just roll, and others just aren't any good. I'd wander around the small room trying to stay out of the way of the nurses. I'd move from one side of his bed to the other just to stay within his sight so he wouldn't think that he was alone. I tried to send a quick text to family and friends and hoped it would go through, but cell service usually isn't very good when you're in the ER. I kept the curtain open and occasionally hung out in the hallway, hoping the doctor would see me and not forget about us. During the last visit, my brother's arms were really flailing as they do when he has a UTI, infection, or kidney stone. I wondered if flailing arms were his body's way of telling him that something is going on somewhere in his body. Kidney stones are said to send half a million people to the ER every year. Well, Father Steve has been one of those half a million people several times. He is very familiar with the world of UTIs, kidney stones, and sepsis. Kidney stones are hard deposits of mineral and acid that stick together and can cause unbearable pain when they are passed through the urinary tract. Fortunately, with his paralysis he cannot feel the pain. Unfortunately, the kidney stones cause him to become very sick, and many times he has become septic because with the inability to feel pain, he cannot tell anyone that there may be a problem. The nurses at his healthcare facility now know that it is time to call the ambulance when confusion and difficulty concentrating set in. These are symptoms that a UTI may be brewing, or he may be septic. I cannot even count the number of times that Father Steve has been septic due to a kidney stone infection. Septic shock is a life-threatening condition caused by severe localized or system-wide infection that requires immediate medical attention. It is nothing to mess around with. His nurses watch his every move to try to notice any irregularities that he is having in a day to avoid this sudden onset of becoming septic.

While in the ER, I would look back and forth in the hallway hoping to make eye contact with someone, anyone. We were both getting anxious and looking for answers. Once, I took my eyes off my brother only for a few minutes, and when I looked back at him, he was covered in blood. The IV site came undone, probably because of his constant movement. The IV site was in his left arm, causing blood to drip down all over the floor. As his left arm flailed, blood splattered all over the wall to the right of him. His face was covered in blood, and so was the blanket. The IV bag was spilling all over the floor. I yelled for help and went to hold his arm down to prevent more blood from splattering on the wall as I stood in the blood on the floor. The nurse came in, found a new IV site, and put tape around the site to avoid this from happening again. I washed the blood from his face, and the nurse got him a new blanket. Soon he was ready to go for a CAT scan.

A cleaning lady peeked in his room, as she made her way down the hallway. She asked if she could come in and clean up the mess. I welcomed her in, and she stood there puzzled. She couldn't understand why blood was on the floor on one side of the room and how it got splattered all over the wall on the other side. I explained the event of the evening, and she cleaned up the room so efficiently. I thanked her, and she left the room clean and sterile like it was before we even came in.

Not all ER visits are as dramatic as this one, but there usually is a story to tell when we get back to the facility. Many of the ER visits lead to a diagnosis of my brother being septic, and usually, he would have to be admitted. He will always have to deal with kidney stones since he is immobile and constantly sitting in the wheelchair. His last visit ended up with him having two kidney stones moving at the same time. The doctor said that it was very rare for that to happen, but if it does, you will need surgery quickly to place stents in for those stones to move. His blood pressure dropped crazy low—like 42/24. I was told by two doctors that if he didn't go to surgery that night, he would not have seen the morning.

Now, this wasn't the first time in my head I thought that it might be time to go out and buy that little black dress because he looked as though he might not make it. I made the decision at that point that a black dress would not be worn by me because if it was God's decision to bring my brother home to him, then that would be a true celebration for my brother not to have to suffer any more.

He was confused and was lying in the bed just constantly looking around. He wasn't looking for me because I was right there. He had to be looking for God because I sure was. I was very scared and just held his hand and prayed. He prayed along with me, which was amazing because he did not respond to any other conversation. I was sure God would show up, but there was a lot going on in the world. There was the chemical spill in East Palestine, Ohio, from a railroad derailment and, of course, the constant war in the Ukraine. How does God choose who he is going to help anyway?

They immediately took him into surgery, and all went well. God did give us a few minutes of his time. It was a quick visit, but a healing visit!

Father Steve spent a few days recovering in the hospital and went back to the nursing facility, the place where many of the following short stories take place. Now off to brighter and more cheerful short stories. Let's put all the medical jargon behind us, and see what Father Steve is up to now.

A BOX OF CHOCOLATES

> This is the day that the Lord has made;
> let us rejoice in it and be glad.
> —Psalm 118:24 (NABRE)

In the movie titled, *Forrest Gump*, Tom Hanks plays the role of a physically and mentally challenged individual. A very famous quote from the movie is Tom Hanks saying, "My momma would always say, 'Life is like a box of chocolates you never know what you're gonna get.'" This saying is very fitting, for what I believe Father Steve's private duty nurses describe the time that they spend with him. They work twelve-hour shifts: 7:00 a.m.–7:00 p.m. and 7:00 p.m.–7:00 a.m.

I can so easily picture the day nurse at 7:00 a.m. They are carrying their box of chocolates and holding on tight. As they open the door, their box of chocolates immediately opens. Just as they are not sure what filling they will get snuggled inside of their piece of chocolate; they never know what their 7:00 a.m.–7:00 p.m. shift will bring with Father Steve. It was now time for them to pick out their chocolate. Will they pick a caramel, strawberry, orange, raspberry, coconut, fruit, or nougat-filled chocolate? Any of these chocolates would mean that it would be a pretty good day. My brother would have a decent appetite and might even join in the activity room with the other patients on this day. His physical therapy would go smoothly, nothing remarkable, but smooth. It's a calm day for him and his nurse.

The ultimate pick for the day nurse would be the chocolate-covered cherry. They really smile now because they know what this means. They picture in their head their favorite two scoop sundae or even a banana split covered in their favorite syrup with whipped cream, nuts and the cherry on the top. This means that life couldn't be better, and Father Steve's day would be the best ever. They hit the jackpot! He would have a healthy day. His blood pressure would stay regulated. He wouldn't have any aches or pains, and he would have a peaceful sense about himself. His day would begin with his favorite eight o'clock coffee and the local newspaper. The morning would go smoothly with no hiccups. Dressing and transferring out of bed would not be problematic and go fluently. His physical therapy session would end with rewards of achievement because he either tackled a new exercise or exceeded his goals with an old one. His lunch and supper would go smoothly because he would have a great appetite. He may now even go for a ride just to get some fresh air. He would finish his day with some correspondence with family and friends. Now all this was great because his nurse picked the best chocolate in the box.

What happens when the day nurse picks the bittersweet piece of chocolate? They almost want to put it back or throw it away. They know that this means that Father Steve will have to suck it up and figure out how to make it through the day just like they will. It won't be a pleasant day at all. In fact, it will be tough. There will be no interest in the newspaper, and his morning coffee won't even sound good to him. His appetite would not be very good, and he'll be uncomfortable with various aches and pains. Spending the day in bed may be all he wants. Hopefully, a hospital visit won't be included in this day. At the end of the day, Father Steve and his nurse both feel like they made it through the day by the grace of God.

Now it is time for the shift change.

It's 7:00 p.m., and it was time for the day nurse to leave. They greet the night nurse at the door. They go over a few notes from the day and wait for the night nurse to open their box and pick out their chocolate. They hope that the night nurse picks the sweet delicious one and hopes for a good night for Father Steve and the nurse. They close their box of chocolates, close the door behind them, and won't open their box of candy until their next shift.

If the night nurse picks a chocolate-covered strawberry, orange, raspberry, coconut, or nougat-filled candy they will now have a pretty good night with Father Steve. He will probably have a nighttime snack, listen to some good music, and have a fairly peaceful night. He may have a few aches or pains, but nothing too uncomfortable for him. It won't be a totally restless evening, but not perfectly restful either. Morning will come, and he will feel decently rested.

If the night nurse picks the chocolate-covered cherry, the nurse is smiling and knows that Father Steve is in for the best night of his life, and so are they. This makes his male nurse especially happy because he will be in for a great night for pizza and a football game. It's their thing. After the game, soft music or the sound of rain would be played on his iPad for him to fall asleep. There won't be any aches and pains the whole night. He will sleep through the whole night even while they turn him every two hours. He would wake up well rested and ready for whatever the next day has to offer. Talk about a blue-ribbon night!

Unfortunately, there is a chance that the night nurse could pick the bittersweet chocolate candy. This would mean a very restless night was ahead for the nurse and my brother, almost sleepless. It would probably consist of aches and pains and a lot of uncomfortableness. It would be a long night for the both of them. It would be a night that they would want to end quickly but knew it wouldn't. It would turn out to be like a never-ending night, and they both would wait for the morning light.

Now, come the real-life days for us. Most of our days are the typical chocolate-covered caramel, strawberry, orange, raspberry, coconut, fruit, or nougat-filled candy day. These days go typically fine for us. Work goes well, life seems to be normal, and everyone in our family is okay. We don't get any phone calls with news that would disturb our day. It's a partly sunny, partly cloudy day outside and is not too hot and not too cold—just your average day. We are pretty happy with God!

Every now and then, we get blessed with a chocolate-covered cherry day. It's the best day ever! Even if it's not a sunny day, it's going to be a good day! You might go on a new adventure or learn a new skill, something you've always wanted to do, but were never gutsy enough to try. Everyone is getting along, and your workday flies by. If you are looking for work, you might finally find employment, maybe get a well-deserved pay raise that you worked so hard for, meet the love of your life or maybe even find out you're having a baby. These are faith-filled joyful days when it's easy to love God!

Now comes the bittersweet chocolate days. These are the hard days when nothing goes as planned. You lose your job or maybe not get the job that you thought you interviewed so well for. You get bad health news about yourself or a loved one. Your children come home with some troubling news, or maybe in the worst-case scenario: they don't come home at all. These bittersweet days almost make it impossible for you to find God. Your faith is now challenged. He'll get you through those bittersweet chocolate days. You will be amazed at the strength you will encompass. You might not always get the best outcome, but God will be there right beside you and he will get you through those days!

It is now time for you to remember those chocolate-covered caramel, strawberry, orange, raspberry, coconut, fruit, or nougat-filled candy days when you knew that God was at your side.

How about the chocolate-covered cherry day when he literally carried you through the whole day. You felt like you were flying!

However, we all must always remember that the bittersweet chocolate days can and will change when the sun rises the next day. It may bring you the chocolate-covered cherry days with syrup, whipped cream and nuts. Don't forget the cherry on top! Enjoy that day and praise God for it. They'll be more of them to come, I promise!

APPALACHIA MISSION MINISTRY

> When you give, give generously and not with a stingy heart; for that, the Lord your God, will bless you in all your works and undertakings. The land will never lack for needy persons; that is why I command you: "Open your hand freely to your poor and to your needy kin in your land."
> —Deuteronomy 15:10–11 (NABRE)

Father Steve was a part of the Father Beiting Appalachian Mission Center and had been going to Harlan County, Kentucky, for the five years preceding his accident.

Father Steve's last trip for this missionary work was when he worked at St. Paul's church. He packed up a van full of adult and teenager volunteers. Before they set off on their mission, St. Paul's church was asked to help donate some of the things that the volunteers would need for themselves such as paper products, cleaning products, and lots of snacks to get through the week. When the van was ready to take off, it was packed with many items that people so graciously and generously provided for them. Gifts of money were also provided so that the volunteers could buy food to cook for the week. They were then ready to go to do some missionary work!

Father Steve and the volunteers helped with cement work, painted houses, and installed drywall and other construction projects for the needy. They also worked on electrical and plumbing projects and some landscaping. There were numerous rattlesnakes in the area, so volunteers needed to be careful when working outside. Most of the work was focused inside the homes. They were also able to work in a trailer that needed various improvements inside. The people who lived in the houses or trailers stayed in them while all the workers helped to improve their homes. They were extremely grateful watching the volunteers work so hard to give them a good place to live. On a typical trip, they would work on at least two to three different families' houses. There was a lot of work that needed to be done.

Some of the volunteers even spent their own money to buy cat and dog food because the people in the homes had pets and they didn't have sufficient funds to feed them. While they were there, some of the volunteers stayed at the dorms of the church; and if there were too many of them, others stayed at the local motel. The women who went down there would cook the meals and wash the shirts every day for the people to wear. They were able to eat three meals a day. Some of the teenagers would pack up their lunch and take it with them, but other times, they were able to come back and eat in the cafeteria.

When their work was done, they would get to do something exciting. One day, they went to the coal mine and rode in the little carts and learned all about the activities that were done in the mines. It was an educational and a fun experience for all of them. Sometimes, they even went to a little shopping center for some shopping. When they were finished and their time was over after a week, a new crew would come down for the next week.

My husband, Mike, was able to join Father Steve on a mission journey. He loved the work that he did there and came home with the address of a family that needed a lot of help. We sent them clothes and school supplies for the fall, and the family was extremely grateful. The girls in the family even wrote and sent thank-you notes to Mike and me.

A newly constructed pavilion was built in honor of Father Steve after his accident. During the ribbon-cutting ceremony for the pavilion, it was decided that it would be called the Amen Pavilion. The pavilion was constructed by a group of teenage volunteers from the Diocese of Youngstown. Father Steve was contacted to tell him all about the pavilion since he couldn't make the visit there, and he responded, "I'm so excited about the work that has been done there in Harlan County. As far as the groups coming down to Harlan County for the summer, that is definitely a spirit-filled place, evangelism working overtime. My heart is with all of you for all the hard work and dedication of so many people and working in so many different facets. Please keep me in your prayers."

Amen Pavilion will serve as a community gathering place for dinners, picnics, or just a place to sit down and have fellowship together. A fire pit was also constructed near the pavilion, which is available for public use in gathering events. Also, on the first Thursday of every month, a free food pantry is available to senior citizens at St. Stephen Church in Cumberland, Kentucky. On the third Thursday of every month, the pantry is available to everyone else who is in need.

HURRICANE KATRINA

Do nothing out of selfishness or out of vainglory; rather, humbly regard others as more important than yourselves, each looking out not for his own interests, but [also] everyone for those of others.
—Philippians 2:3–4 (NABRE)

Hurricane Katrina was a devastating category 5 Atlantic hurricane that resulted in 1,392 fatalities and caused damage estimated between $97.4 billion to $145.5 billion in late August 2005, particularly in the city of New Orleans and its surrounding areas. This hurricane developed winds in excess of 156 miles per hour.

After it made landfall in Louisiana on August 29, Hurricane Katrina produced widespread flooding in southeastern Louisiana because the levee system that held back the waters of Lake Pontchartrain and Lake Borgne were completely overwhelmed by ten inches of rain and Katrina's storm surge. The levee was built to contain the flow of water and protect residents and developed properties. On this day, the levee failed.

Repairing Hurricane Katrina's damage leveled out in January 2007, putting the primary recovery period at about eighteen months after the storm. This is why the following story takes place.

Father Steve, who was pastor of Immaculate Heart of Mary, in Austintown, Ohio, at the time, was approached to gather some adults and eighth graders together to make a journey to Louisiana to help with building homes and visiting some of the people that lost their homes in Louisiana. They gathered for a trip that would happen in June of 2007 to the ninth ward of New Orleans, Louisiana. The ninth ward was truly devastated because it was a vulnerable, poor ward where many residents did not have the money to invest in anything that would protect them from a hurricane or strong storms.

It was easy for Father Steve to find some volunteers for this project because it was never easy to turn down my brother when he asked you for a favor. Plus, they knew what a great ministry they would be doing along with him. Two passenger minivans were packed up with about seven adults and twelve children aged between twelve and thirteen years old. There were seven girls and five boys who were eighth graders of the confirmation class of Immaculate Heart of Mary. The vans were packed up with snacks, cookies, and money that was donated from the parish for the adults and children who went on this trip. Sleeping bags, backpacks, and everything that the children and adults needed were packed up in the vans. The vans were just passenger vans with some hard uncomfortable seats, but everybody bore with it because they knew the trip that they were going on was going to be a faithful trip where they would learn a lot and do God's work. They drove for sixteen hours straight, making just a few necessary stops.

The adults and children stayed at a convent in the middle of the older part of New Orleans. The convent was likely built in the 1800s. They were fed in a cafeteria room by the nuns who also lived there. It was extremely hot and humid with no air conditioning, but no one complained because once again, they knew that they were doing God's work.

They first visited a house that was built by volunteers from the Diocese of Youngstown, Ohio. Their project was a home for a mother named Lydia and her two sons who previously lived in a FEMA trailer. Her two children who were diabetic, had neuropathy in their feet. There was no way to regulate the water temperature in the trailer, so both had feet that were burned because they could not feel how hot the water was. They had a hard time walking as a result of these burns. It was so important that Lydia and her sons would now have a home to live in and not have to worry about the issues of the FEMA trailers.

The work sites at the home were run by Christian organizations led by college students from all over the country. A lot of them were from Baptist colleges and non-Catholic colleges. They weren't Catholic, but hanging around my brother for a week opened their eyes a little bit to our religion. Father Steve did not preach, but just had a way with words to share ecumenical unity while he was there. These college students were the worksite leaders and foremen of the jobs. Some of them were ministers, and the group of people that came from Austintown, Ohio, would be their helpers. They built three stories of scaffolding and did concrete work and any other type of work that was needed to help to make this new home more comfortable for the new owners.

Every day lunches were packed, maybe even by Lydia. A few times, homeless people would come past the house, and Father Steve would engage in conversation with them and share his lunch, maybe even half his sandwich. God tells us in the Bible that when we feed other people, we are feeding him. The twelve- and thirteen-year-olds saw this and began to share their lunches too, without Father Steve saying a word to them. Father Steve made them all feel safe and comfortable. The children learned a lot just by watching my brother. He didn't even have to tell them what to do. They followed his good example, and somehow, they knew they were doing exactly what God wanted them to do.

The adults and teenagers did spend one day of fun and got to visit the French Quarter, which is the area where Mardi Gras takes place. There are many bars and restaurants in this area. They were able to go to Bubba Gump's to eat and visited the Cafe Du Monde where they each enjoyed a beignet, the famous and favorite pastry of New Orleans.

It was recently said by one of the girls who went on this trip that her experience helped shape her teenage years. The children and adults saw a lot of devastation, and when they returned home, they truly realized what they had and were anxious to share their stories with many others. A beautiful setting doing the work of God!

POPE FRANCIS

> And so, I say to you, you are Peter, and upon this rock I will build my church, and the gates of the netherworld shall not prevail against it.
> —Matthew 16:18 (NABRE)

Right after my brother's accident, I decided that I needed some inspiration from a higher authority. I bothered God constantly, so I figured that I would leave him alone for a while. Lots of other people needed him too, so I'm sure that a break from me was welcomed by God. I decided that it couldn't hurt to try and reach out to Pope Francis. I guess that I pictured the pope sitting in the Vatican waiting on some mail from me.

I obtained an address for the pope, sat down, and wrote a beautiful letter to him. I'm not sure what I expected the pope to do, but a few short prayers from him would suffice.

My letter was answered, not by the pope, but by the pope's United States personal representative, Archbishop Carlo Maria Viganò. I received his response in a very timely manner on the day before Christmas Eve 2013. I was so excited I screamed and cried to the point where my children who were visiting me thought I had won the lottery. When they realized what I received, they knew in their hearts that to me it was much better than the lottery.

I wanted to reach out to the pope and tell him all about Father Steve, his tragedy, and his past and present ministry. The pope has been known to wash the feet of prisoners; Father Steve was in his accident on the way to celebrate the Mass and visit with prisoners, so of course I felt like they would have a connection. Father Steve washed the feet of parishioners on many Holy Thursdays during

Lent. I sent the pope some pictures of my brother and how his chalice and ciborium were crushed in the accident. I also sent a picture of my brother distributing ashes on my husband's forehead on Ash Wednesday. In another picture, that I sent to the pope, Father Steve is sitting in the center of a circle of people at a prayer service. Finally, I sent him a picture showing Father Steve at a funeral giving a homily for an eighteen-year-old girl whom he met at Cleveland Metro and later passed away.

Archbishop Carlo Maria Vigano sent me some pictures of the pope and three pairs of rosary beads that were blessed by the pope. I kept one of the rosary beads, which are pure white; I gave one pair to my brother Father Steve, and the last pair to my youngest brother, John, who helped me get my letter to the pope organized. The rosary beads rest on my nightstand and are there for when I want to pray the rosary to Mary at night. I corresponded back and forth a few more times to the archbishop. I sent him Easter greetings and followed up with updates about Father Steve's condition. He has always responded back to me; it was almost like having a special holy pen pal.

About a year and a half later, the pope was scheduled to come to the United States for a papal visit. He would arrive in Philadelphia and stay from September 25–28, 2015. When I saw this papal visit advertised in our church bulletin, I sent in my deposit to secure a spot for my husband and me.

The trip was amazing and spiritual. We traveled by motor coach, met some wonderful people, and enjoyed every single minute of the trip. We ate well, bought souvenirs, went to the theater to see the musical *Joseph and the Amazing Technicolor Dreamcoat*, and headed to the Festival of Families celebration. The celebration was held in downtown Philadelphia and was an intercultural outdoor public event celebrating Catholic family life with entertainment, activities, and food concessions. The highlight of the trip was on Sunday, September 27, when there was an outdoor papal Mass with Pope Francis. This Mass was attended by hundreds and thousands of fellow Christians who were united in praise and worship. To be able to attend the Mass with the pope presiding and to receive communion on that day was an unbelievable experience for me. When it was time to pray the Our Father, I called my brother so that he could pray this powerful prayer with tens of thousands of devout Catholics at the same time.

During the Festival of Families, the pope made an appearance. Of course, I had a letter written to give him all about Father Steve. I was determined to make a connection with him somehow. The whole area around where the pope was going to appear was fenced off and people tried to push their way up front. We only had one person standing in front of us, so we had an amazing view. I protected my area very well. When you're only four feet, ten inches tall a crowd of people can run you over very quickly. Secret Service agents were stationed all over the place. They were lined up along the fence and on top of buildings and surrounded the pope as he was driven through the streets. How could I get my letter to him under those circumstances? The only chance I had was to climb the fence. My husband spoke no words but gave me the look as is to say, "Don't you dare." I thought maybe I could give it to a Secret Service or a law enforcement person, but they never made eye contact with anyone, let alone spoke with anyone. You could only hear them talk if there was a problem within the crowd. No one appeared to be interested in my letter, but I felt deep down in my heart that the pope and I made some eye contact, and he knew all about my letter. My brother would be taken care of. That was all I needed to make me feel good.

I was able to attend another papal Mass on Easter in 2022 while vacationing in Italy. The two religious papal experiences in my life have been treasured by me.

SHOES

> When I say, "My foot is slipping," your mercy, Lord, holds me up. When cares increase within me, your comfort gives me joy.
> —Psalm 94:18–19 (NABRE)

Gosh, I love shoes! I have shoes for every occasion and holiday. I love it when a new celebration pops up because that gives me a reason to adorn my feet. When life gives you lemons, I don't make lemonade, like the saying goes. I buy a pair of new shoes! Besides an answered prayer, a new pair of shoes can make a bad day turn out just right.

I have high heels, sandals, flip-flops, boots, booties, and tennis shoes. I even own a variety of slippers, and of course, all these come in a variety of colors. When I open my closet, I see a rainbow of color. There—isn't that a great way to start the day!

Two of my sons love shoes, and so does my sister. My middle son, Tony, is so busy with work and family that he feels that there's just no time to be bothered with shoes. He just can't wrap his head around our interest in shoes. He says he's happy when he gets somewhere, looks down, and realizes he didn't forget to put his shoes on. He believes that they're overrated. He apparently didn't inherit my "love for shoes" gene.

I never realized until recently that my brother has quite an interest in shoes. I guess that there is such a thing as a "love for shoes" gene. It's very sad and ironic that a man who hasn't walked in almost ten years has so many pairs of shoes. His shoes always look like they're brand-new. That is obviously because they've never hit the ground. There is not one speck of dust or dirt on the bottom of his shoes.

His choice of shoes comes in two categories, dress shoes and tennis shoes. Most of his shoes are geared around his ministry in the Catholic Church. Father Steve wears green tennis shoes, symbolizing growth and new life, during ordinary time in the Catholic church. Ordinary time has two parts, but it remains one season. The first part begins right after the feast of the Epiphany and runs until Tuesday, the day before Ash Wednesday. The second part begins the Monday after Pentecost and runs until the First Sunday of Advent. My brother's white shoes symbolize joy, purity, victory, and grace. These will be worn at Easter and funerals to celebrate the Resurrection of Jesus Christ and at Christmas to celebrate his birth. Purple shoes are worn during the Lenten season because purple reflects sorrow, penance, suffering, preparation and sacrifice. Red shoes are worn to symbolize the Feast of Pentecost in the Catholic Church. Red reminds us of the fire of the Holy Spirit. His blue tennis shoes are worn during the Advent season, representing preparation, penitence, and royalty. Also, blue is worn in honor of Mary to represent modesty, devotion to motherhood, and how Mary is blessed by the divinity of Heaven. Black shoes are worn for dress occasions. Beige tennis shoes are worn during exercise and physical therapy sessions. Lastly, orange is worn for fun, fall, Halloween, and Thanksgiving.

While we can all enjoy the various places our shoes take us, my brother cannot. My brother cannot enjoy the pleasure of putting on a pair of flip flops and letting the sand that blankets the beaches warm up his feet. He can't even wear those same flip flops and feel the peaceful blue ocean water cool down his warm feet. My, how we take things for granted! He doesn't have the pleasure of taking a walk in the first snowfall of the season and won't hear the crunch of the snow. The beautiful blanket of snow glistening in the sun and looking like God sprinkled glitter from heaven on it will never be marked by my brother's footprints again. He won't even ever get to make a snow angel like he did when he was a little kid. A walk in the rain under an umbrella can even be fun, and it is a must if you enjoy a little tranquil time to yourself on a day when it's drizzling. As you walk in the rain, the air will smell clean and fresh. A burst of colorful flowers and greenery might appear on your walk reminding you that this wouldn't be possible without the rain and the help of our God. This is another very simple experience he can't enjoy. It really isn't fair at all is it? When he left the hospital, he was reminded that everything would be okay, he just needed to make some adjustments in his life. Is it possible to adjust to never setting your feet down on the ground again?

Father Steve has yet to complain about the fact that all these shoes will never even take him for a walk. He never questions why, but he accepts God's plan for him.

Since shoes won't get my brother to the places he needs to be, he now relies on the black tires of his electric wheelchair on his journey. This chair has taken him to some sad but also some fun places. When he can't get to these places solely by way of his wheelchair, he gets in his wheelchair-accessible van. The most important place that this van takes him is to various churches in the surrounding area where he can continue to perform his ministry. So where did this van come from? Who has friends that would purchase a wheelchair-accessible van for you to travel in since you had no means of transportation except to call an ambulette to take you wherever you needed to go? Well, Father Steve has two of them. A great friend of my brother who loves to meditate, pray with Father Steve, and talk about spirituality with him pulled through with his generosity. His friend's brother, another very generous man, helped to purchase a beautiful new van for Father Steve to make his life so much easier. This van has taken him to so many places and brought him countless days of enjoyment.

My brother often has doctor appointments that may be an hour or so from his current residence. While visiting a doctor in the Cleveland area, there are times when he'll drive that wheelchair down to the street to catch a hot dog from the local food vendor. Other times, the wheelchair will take him to a fancier restaurant where we will all enjoy a great meal. By the time we leave the restaurant, he has already made friends with the waitresses. We'll meet the most patient people who are waiting on him, and they often want to hear his story. He'll always share it and always takes the time to learn a little bit about them too.

One fun visit that the wheelchair took him on was a trip to a Vince Gill concert. Father Steve is a big fan of his, and we were honored to get to meet him after the show. Vince signed a T-shirt for him and gave Father Steve the ultimate respect as he talked to him. Carrie Underwood came to town, and we were able to get some good seats to see her also. One of Father Steve's favorite songs by Carrie Underwood is, "Jesus, Take the Wheel." It really resonates with him. On November 13, 2013, it did not seem that Jesus took the wheel of the white Pontiac Grand Am that my brother drove. No one could believe what had happened that day. Now that time has passed, we realized that Jesus did take the wheel of his car, or my brother wouldn't be here with us today.

A sad place that Father Steve's wheelchair takes him is to the hospital to pray for and visit sick patients. He has occasionally been called to go and anoint the sick and dying. I have been with him on some of those occasions. Because of his wheelchair, he has not been able to get close enough to patients in the hospital to perform the anointing of the sick without help. He would say the appropriate prayers and instruct me on how to use the sacred oils on the hands of the patients. It is a very intense but beautiful moment for the patients, their families, and me. I am honored to be a part of that little service, and the families are so very appreciative. Funeral homes are another sad visit for Father Steve, which brings tearful eyes to say goodbye to a family member or friend. His prayers are always welcomed.

During the COVID-19 outbreak, a patient where my brother lives was not doing well and was suffering from COVID-19. He was close to death, and it was not safe for my brother to go into his room because the virus was so contagious. It was raining outside, but the only way for this patient to receive his last blessing was through the window. In the rain, my brother maneuvered his wheelchair and got to the patient's window, where he prayed and blessed the patient through the window. I was reminded the other day by the son of the dying patient how eternally grateful the family was for what Father Steve did that day.

There is a lake in front of the church where my brother last resided, and he loved to fish there. He still visits this lake, trying to maneuver his chair around to get to a good fishing spot. When he got the assignment as pastor of St. Paul's, I told my sons that Father Steve would be at a parish with a lake located in the front of it and a Dairy Queen behind it. They knew his love for fishing and the Dairy Queen, and they asked if Father Steve died and went to heaven. Fishing is probably like heaven on earth for my brother.

At his facility, he mostly enjoys his time outside wheeling around the perimeter of the facility. It's a great place for him to have visitors, relax in the sun, have a snack, take a nap, or feed the chipmunks. We spend a lot of time outdoors with him because it is so very peaceful. I try to leave when he's not looking because I feel so guilty walking away when he can't use his legs. It might sound silly, but it's my thing.

Yes, the wheelchair gets him where he needs to be. If you asked me if my brother has accepted his life in his wheelchair, I would have to say "No," but that's okay. I think if he accepted his life in a wheelchair, it would be like he was done trying and giving up. I feel he still has faith, hope, trust, and determination. This is what gets him through his days. It works for him, and it works for me too.

THE BLUE LIGHT SPECIAL

> Then God said: Let there be light, and there
> was light. God saw that the light was good.
> God then separated the light from the darkness.
> —Genesis 1:3–4 (NABRE)

There was a favorite store in my neighborhood years ago that everybody frequented. This popular store was called Kmart, where hourly specials were the exciting feature of the store. My brother loved shopping in the store because at one point it was located three minutes from the parish rectory where he lived for fifteen years. It is also where the blue light made its popular appearance. It was first introduced as red until the fire department informed them that a red light might indicate to the customers that they needed to search for an emergency exit. The light was changed to blue and was popular beginning in 1965 until 1991.

While you were shopping you would hear a siren and a surprise announcement with somebody blaring into the loudspeaker. Their message was, "Attention, Kmart shoppers!" At that moment, shoppers literally rushed searching for the pole that supported the iconic blue light. A lot of commotion was going on when the siren went off as customers scanned the store looking for what might be their exciting new bargain of the day. When that blue light rotated, you stopped looking at what you were presently shopping for because you knew the blue light would bring you a better bargain. The blue light sale lasted for fifteen minutes. The prices of over thirty thousand items were reduced throughout the existence of the novelty of the blue light.

Father loved the blue light special just as every other customer did. Little did he know that a blue light would appear again in his life thirty-plus years later. This blue light wouldn't stand for a special bargain in the store, but for a special priest who needed many prayers. The congregation at Saint Paul's parish where my brother was the pastor prior to his accident, lit a blue vigil lamp in church for his support. This blue lamp was a reminder for the parishioners to pray for his recovery. The parish asked people to show a visible sign by installing a blue light bulb in their porch lamp, porch light, lamppost, or in their welcome candles in the windows. Another idea of support came from a person telling others to tie a blue ribbon or bow around their lamppost, fence, or tree. The parish asked for people to show their support for their parish priest regardless of their religious or nonreligious beliefs. The parish secretary sent out postcards alerting the community to show their support for Father Steve through the blue light project. Blue bows made by a parishioner were displayed in and outside the church. One woman made blue ribbons for the parishioners to wear for their support for my brother. The mayor of New Middletown, a parishioner of St. Paul's, called it "the blue light special." How ironic is that? At one point in Father Steve's life, the Kmart light brought him to a special deal. Now the special deal was for him, a humble and sincere priest who constantly prayed for his parishioners. It was the ultimate time for everyone to repay him for all that he did for them by praying and supporting him. The parishioners described Father Steve as being a sincere, humble, and good man who loved the Lord. I'm not surprised at all by the continued love and support that comes from Saint Paul's Parish. It is a close-knit parish where the parishioners have each other's backs and won't give up on praying for their pastor's return to health. Blue lights are still seen in the town and the neighboring communities.

Last Sunday as I attended Mass, I heard and sang the song "Christ, Be Our Light," written by Bernadette Farrell. In this song, Bernadette tells us to be servants to one another. Saint Paul's Parish consists of these servants who united to pray for their leader. The refrain of this song is powerful and reminds us of who should be our real light, as we all sing together, "Christ, Be Our Light." I sing this song from my heart as I live the words, and I love how the words relate to my life.

As I sit and write this little story, I look outside. Living in northeast Ohio, the temperature is thirty-five degrees, but it feels like twenty-eight degrees. It's chilly, and I watch the snowfall come down and start to accumulate. Snow is one of my favorite things in the world. It looks like a great time to go for a walk and listen to the song "Christ, Be Our Light." Snow is clean and white and is a sign of purity. Snow can represent truth, peace, and relaxation. It is considered to be a sign of life and can represent a new beginning that lies ahead. Can my brother get his new beginning filled with good health and happiness? Only God knows. Eventually, the snow will melt, and I won't be happy, but melting snow can often symbolize the dissolving of fears and problems in real life. Now that's a nice thought for the day. Who doesn't want their fears and problems dissolved?

The Garden of Hope at Liberty Healthcare Center.

THE GARDEN OF HOPE

> As the earth brings forth its shoots, and a garden makes
> its seeds spring up, So will the Lord God make justice
> spring up, and praise before all the nations.
> —Isaiah 61:11 (NABRE)

Do you enjoy facing the sun and feeling its warmth? Do you enjoy positive vibes and feeling pure happiness? If you answer yes to those questions, then your needs are much like that of a sunflower.

As my brother sat outside in the parking lot of the health care facility where he resides, he looked out to the stone wall and commented that he believed sunflowers would sure look pretty planted there. In the morning, all sunflowers face east, the direction of the rising sun. As the sun moves, so will the sunflower heads, until fall when they are too big and heavy. He, too, wanted to be like the sunflower. He wanted to face the sun, sit back, and bask in the warmth of the sun. Since the accident, his body has a hard time regulating his body temperature, and he likes the feeling of being warm. Being cold or even the least bit chilly makes him feel like little needles are pricking him. The warmth of the sun makes him feel like he's wrapped in a fleece blanket. I think he felt that surrounding himself with sunflowers would do the same trick. Traditionally, sunflowers are a sign of positivity, happiness, cheer, good luck, health, devotion, hope, and faithfulness. Between the warmth of the sun and all the attributes of the sunflower, my brother feels that he is all set.

The director of the nursing facility gave Father Steve permission to plant a garden. The smile on his face was priceless! The initial row of sunflowers that we started with eventually turned into two gardens with a cement walkway between them. This cement walkway was wide enough for a wheelchair. At first, the garden did not have a cement walkway. If it rained earlier in the day and was muddy in the grass, my brother and other wheelchair-bound people could not go anywhere near the gardens because of the muddy grass. The cement walkway now allows them to ride right up to the gardens and plant themselves among the planted flowers and vegetables. I love to plant, and the thought of filling up two gardens with vibrant flowers and vegetable plants put a smile on my face too. Now I not only have flower gardens at my home to plant in, but two big empty plots of dirt waiting for me to do my magic and turn them into a massive burst of color that not only looks beautiful but smells pretty too. We have planted many rows of sunflowers along with petunias, marigolds, dahlias, vincas, impatiens, daisies, geraniums, begonias, coleus, and black-eyed Susans. Large hanging baskets are planted in the ground, allowing them to spread throughout the flowers. Perennials have been added to the garden that come up every spring. A mass of color shows up in a few months after planting.

My husband works just as hard as I do in the garden. He works a small tiller to get it ready, while a friend of one of Father Steve's nurses brings in a big rototiller to help. Mike rakes, installs fences to keep the bunnies out, and carries bags of peat moss and dirt out of his truck. He is wonderful at pleasing my brother and me. It is fun going out and shopping for flowers and vegetable plants, waiting for a beautiful day, and planting everything. Many friends and family members often send him gifts of money. Some of this money is used to purchase all the beautiful flowers and vegetable plants. So many of you have helped to make his garden a delightful place. Thank you again! A relative loved tomato plants and was great at producing the very best tomatoes. He had a special place to plant those tomato plants in that garden. Father Steve loves potatoes and greens beans, so we started planting them. In the past, we added cherry tomatoes, peppers, zucchini, eggplants, cabbage, squash, and pumpkins. We even had fun planting peanuts. For some reason, I assumed that they would come up dry, roasted, and salted. I now had raw peanuts to try. What would we do with all this food? Before COVID-19, a basket was placed inside the center of the residence and visitors and workers were encouraged to help themselves.

The garden became a nice little hangout for many people. It is my brother's favorite place to be. Employees, visitors, and the residents enjoy watching the colorless pile of dirt turn into a beautiful mass of color. A black wrought-iron bench was placed between the two gardens as a relaxation spot for anyone who wants a quiet place to relax. The bees, butterflies, birds, and chipmunks pretty much kept to themselves and kept pretty quiet too. You'll only hear the wind chimes on breezy days. There was one summer when most people's gardens did not thrive at all because of the weather we had in the area. The Garden of Hope, as my brother's garden is called, had no problem prospering, and we all often wondered if he would sneak out there and bless it with his holy water. My husband bought Father Steve a special hose for him to use so that he can join in to care for the garden.

Father Steve watering The Garden of Hope

My brother has suggested that this year we add a rock garden. I don't know a thing about a rock garden, but I will do some research so that I can make it as pretty as possible for him. A solar-powered fountain was purchased for his garden, and it will run for four hours, mainly from 12:00 p.m. until 4:00 p.m. These are the hours where most of the residents sit outside to enjoy the garden and the summer weather.

In the fall time, the Garden of Hope is transformed into a fall wonderland. Perennials and flowers that are still blooming are left alone, while dead flowers are cleared away. Mums, pumpkins, scarecrows, along with cornstalks and haystacks are brought in and many other decorations are strategically placed. During Thanksgiving, turkeys and pilgrims are added to the garden.

The nursing facility has a fall festival, and Father suggested maybe an outdoor Mass would be fun. The outdoor Mass turned into a toe-tapping polka Mass. A polka band, starring Eddie Vallus, played religious songs with the polka beat. The sound of the drums, accordion, guitar, and cymbals were heard all the way down the block. A little over two hundred people attended this fall event. Programs with song selections were printed and distributed to friends, relatives, employees, residents, and their families. When Mass concluded, a raffle was held for people to win the mums, and fall decorations that were placed in front of the altar as decorations. It was a time of praying, singing, fun, and peace for all and was a beautiful way to end the fall season with warm weather. We were blessed with that warm weather because we knew that our fall season in northeast Ohio could come to a halt sooner than later.

There is a cross at the entrance of the garden that was given to him from a cousin. This Garden of Hope has also turned into a prayer garden. Many days I find myself praying there whether I am watering the garden, planting, or just relaxing. Many times I would see my brother sitting in the garden, eyes closed, and letting the sun work its warm magic. Father Steve placed a Saint Francis statue at the front of one of the gardens which is a great place for a St. Francis statue because he is the patron saint of all living creatures. Many little bunnies and chipmunks scamper in and out as birds and butterflies fly by.

Sometimes, I'll pull up in my little Saturn and just sit and watch Father Steve. My mom gave me her Saturn when she passed away in 2011 because she said I drove her everywhere she needed to be. I would have been happy if it had only lasted me for a few years, but twelve years later, it is still going strong. It's twenty-three years old with minimal miles on it because two women only drove it around town. I have a brand-new car sitting in my garage, but for some reason I love to take the Saturn. I think it's because I know a part of my mom and dad are with me almost like they're giving me a big hug, especially when I'm having a rough day. I keep my dad's prayer book in the glove box and a little angel pin that my mom gave me next to his prayer book. Our dad passed away in 1993, and our mother passed away in 2011.

I sit and wonder if the old Father Steve would ever come back to us one day? I again find myself searching for the brother that I once knew. How long would I have to wait until I found my brother? I miss that loud and vibrant voice. The voice that let you know that he was there and something dynamic was going to happen. What is this new normal and why do we have to accept it? What would happen if we didn't accept it? I wanted to ask others if they'd seen him, but then I wondered what they would think of me. So I just keep quiet and sit and watch my brother.

I watch and wonder to myself what exactly was he praying for? I wouldn't dare ask him though, because I felt that certain prayers were private. Was he praying asking for a miracle for him to be able to walk? Or was he praying for strength to be able to get through the rest of that day? Would his prayers get answered? I read that God always answers your prayers, but in his own time and in his own way. Would God's way be the same way my brother was expecting? Would God's answers come at a time when my brother least expected it with an answer that maybe was even much better than the request my brother had put in? God does work in mysterious ways and as far as I'm concerned, the reason all this has even happened remains a mystery to all of us. Why is my life filled with so many questions? At times I feel like a little kid asking so many questions and wondering about so many things.

It might be time for me to give God a break. I've always reached out to St. Anthony of Padua, who was a powerful Franciscan preacher, teacher, and the patron saint of lost and stolen articles. Well, Father Steve certainly isn't an article, and he certainly isn't small, like the articles that St. Anthony has helped me find in the past. I've often reached out to him to help me find a memento from someone that was lost, a piece of jewelry that was given to me by an important person in my life that I couldn't find, or that lost piece of paper that had an important phone number or message written on it that I really needed. If he could help me find all of these small but important articles, how could he not help out in the search for my brother? My brother was described recently by an individual as an earthquake. How could St. Anthony not spot this earthquake as he travels around, searching for everything that people have lost, helping those who have reached out to him for his assistance? I should very soon get some results as St. Anthony has joined God in the search for my brother.

WATER

> Jesus answered and said to her, "Everyone who drinks this water will be thirsty again; but whoever drinks the water I shall give will never thirst; the water I shall give will become in him a spring of water welling up to eternal life."
> —John 4:13–14 (NABRE)

In the Bible, water symbolizes faith, salvation, and provision. As water is essential to our physical living, Jesus is essential to our spiritual living. Water has always played an important role in Father Steve's life. His life began by being baptized, and still to this day, he baptizes babies. Holy water is important in his life. Holy water is water that has been blessed by a member of the clergy and is used in baptism. This blessed water is also used to bless individuals, churches, homes, and articles of devotion.

Besides baptizing babies, blessing people, articles, and buildings, Father Steve has used water at all his Holy Thursday celebrations. The washing of the feet is traditionally done on Holy Thursday. This practice copies that of Jesus on the night before he died when he washed the feet of his disciples.

On Father Steve's trip to the Holy Land, many years ago, he was able to bring back some water from the river Jordan where Jesus was baptized by John the Baptist.

A polar bear plunge is an event held during the winter where participants enter a body of water despite the low temperatures of winter. One winter, my brother decided to find some friends who would join him in this polar bear plunge in January. To get himself prepared for this polar bear plunge, he got himself all fired up by taking very cold showers. I don't think any cold shower could prepare anyone for what was in store for Father Steve and his friends in the chilly waters of northeast Ohio in January. The polar bear plunge was held in Mosquito Lake which lies in Bazetta and Mecca townships in the center of Trumbull County. Money that is raised from this event is used for a special cause. The money from this particular event was raised for the Special Olympics.

After my brother's accident, water once again played an important part in his life. He was able to enjoy water therapy at a close-by facility, and it was probably one of his favorite forms of exercise. The warm ninety-degree therapeutic water temperature made his whole body feel better. It was relaxing and comfortable. Whoever helped him in the pool would say the same thing. The warm water helped to ease tension and pain in his body. He was out of his chair and finally had some freedom. My brother would very carefully be moved from his wheelchair to a shower chair. He was then pushed out onto the floor over the pool. The floor would then be lowered slowly into the pool and continuously drop until it reached the bottom of the pool.

There were two therapists who worked in the pool with him. My husband also started to help in the water and a few of my brother's friends joined in. It took several people to be able to accomplish this task. You had to be very careful handling him because you needed to ensure that he wouldn't fall or end up with any skin issues.

Each water therapy session was a learning session for him. Exercises were used to strengthen and train his muscles. He would do forward and backward arm strokes. He would hold five-pound weights while doing these exercises. Three pool noodles were used to keep him afloat. A life preserver was used, but he was uncomfortable with it. Eventually, he was weaned from all the pool noodles. The goal was to help him gain core strength so he would be able to hold himself up and to help with transferring himself from his bed to his wheelchair. He would do sit-ups in the water and use a stick to hit a ball while someone out of the pool would catch it. He was challenged at every session to improve his last time or number of exercises that he did.

Father Steve would do crunches in the water, and he had to do the backstroke against the jets of the pool. There was a camera in the pool, and we were able to watch any activity that was taking place in the water. Father loved floating in the pool water where he said, "It's a powerful moment for me. I float and say, 'Lord, here I am.'" Unfortunately, after about two years of intense water therapy, COVID-19 surfaced and put an end to nursing home visits and water therapy sessions.

Water is so very important to the body and ever so important to him right now. He frequently gets UTIs, so drinking plenty of water can help reduce his risk of them recurring. Maybe the next time you enjoy a glass of water, you can toast to Father Steve for some good health!

WHO'S THE REAL ANGEL HERE?

> For he commands his angels with regard to you, to guard you wherever you go. With their hands they shall support you, lest you strike your foot against a stone.
> —Psalm 91:11–12 (NABRE)

Angels are sent by God to protect us and help us inherit his full kingdom. The Bible tells us that angels are God's servants, carrying out his will and work for our good. An angel is defined as a messenger from God and a guardian of human beings who is represented with wings and wearing a robe. Tanya Carroll Richardson writes about guardian angels and feels that the song "I'll Stand by You," written by Chrissie Hynde, depicts our guardian angels. I really agree with her because our guardian angels do exactly what that song says.

I believe that God gives us all guardian angels, and I also believe that we have guardian angels right here on earth—ones that we can see, touch, and communicate with. They are all around us all the time. Some of them we know very well, but some of them are complete strangers.

I've been approached by many people throughout the last ten years. So many friends, relatives and even strangers have told me that I am an angel because of the good care that I give to my brother. Well, I don't have wings, but walking around in a comfortable robe sounds very darn tempting.

Since his accident, I've been taking care of my brother's clothes and food and keeping him physically comfortable. Before COVID-19, during church services at his residence, I was the Eucharist minister to families, friends, employees, and residents. When I distributed the Eucharist to the residents, they would often look me right in the eyes. I often prayed for them when I got home, realizing that they didn't choose to be in a helpless situation and that someday I may also be in their shoes. If that day comes, I will want somebody to take care of me and bring me the Eucharist too. I made sure he had enough host and wine for the service. I've also helped to distribute ashes on Ash Wednesday. I make sure that his church clothes are washed for the service and are pressed and presentable.

My response to the people who would put angel wings on me, is that my brother would do the same for me. In my mind, my brother seems to be more of an angel to me than I am to him.

He on the other hand, has taught me how to live a faith-filled life through his good example. He gives me spiritual books to read, which results in some great conversations. My husband, nurse, Father Steve, and I have movie time in his room and watch DVDs of *The Chosen*. When we watch *The Chosen*, it is a special time. Father Steve usually likes to watch this DVD at 3:00 p.m., the time that Jesus died. The lights are out and it is quiet time. During these movies, we'll have a snack, but nothing crunchy or noisy. There's absolutely no talking during this time unless you have an extremely important question about the movie. As I sit and watch the movie, I find myself watching my brother too. He never eats during the movie, and his eyes never leave the screen. He loves watching the episode about Jesus and the little children, and his favorite is the story of the disciples fishing. We have all watched it with him a few times. There's something special going on there, and I really can't put my finger on what it is. Sometimes I feel like Father Steve and Jesus make eye contact with each other. It's a very religious and touching moment!

We visit different church services where my brother would celebrate Mass, and I am always inspired by his homilies. He never disappoints his audience. There is a learning experience every time we are together. Either Father Steve has a good quote for the day, a new song, or an article worth sharing. I often feel like he is a teacher, and I am a student. I take care of his physical needs, but he takes care of my spiritual needs.

I retired in 2009 and was able to spend so much time with my mother and Father Steve before she passed away in 2011. God had a great plan for me then. Mike retired at the end of July in 2013. We discussed what we would do with his newfound freedom. We had one grandchild, and we knew that we would spend time with him. After working two jobs for twenty-eight years, my husband finally had the freedom he so well deserved. I told Mike that God would take care of him like he did me when I retired. He would place something in his lap like he did mine. We traveled a little, visiting our children down South and vacationed in Florida. What would fall in our laps on November 13, 2013, would be indescribable.

At times, it looked like Father Steve, and I were both in the running for the title of angel. But I see a candidate in the running who truly deserves the title. I am proud to say my husband, Mike, would be the real winner. He's very humble about what he does for my brother and doesn't like anybody making a big deal about him. Little did my brother know, but when he filled out his emergency contact information, he put in the name of a person who would not only be his emergency contact person, but his guardian angel too. So there he was, the real angel standing right in front of Father Steve and me.

Father Steve's brother-in-law, Mike.

Mike also was raised in a strict Catholic home whose parents were a constant good example of living a faith-filled generous life. They were continually sending clothes to the less fortunate in Appalachia, having a rosary service for friends in their home, or setting out the Christmas Nativity scene at their church. Father Steve was excited that on Mike's dad's ninety-sixth birthday, he was able to bring him a bottle of wine and celebrate the special day with him. He did live to be ninety-eight years old, hoping to make it to one hundred years old. If you needed anything you could go to them, and your wish was granted. Mike's roots are what made him the person that he is today and have turned him into the guardian angel that he is. His parents' names were Angelo and Angeline, so you see, two angels there too!

Mike is truly my and my brother's guardian angel. I must take care of myself and some of my brother's needs, but Mike must take care of himself, my brother and me. He always has quite the job ahead of him because my brother and I can be very needy at times. I need his advice constantly. I need help to decide what to do about certain situations regarding Father Steve's medical needs. He always had the right answers for me. Mike keeps me grounded often and often wipes the tears away from my eyes.

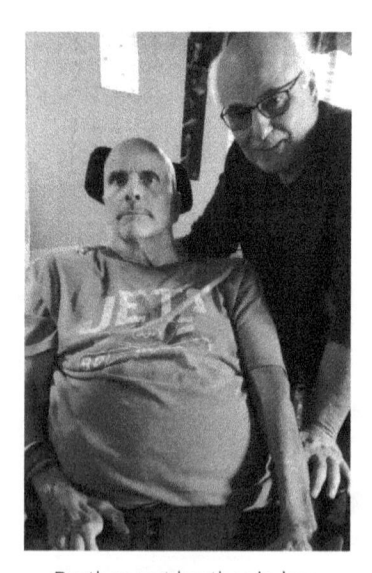

Brother, not brother-in-law.

Mike calls Father Steve *brother* a lot because *in-law* after the word *brother* means nothing to him. Mike doesn't have a brother, so Father Steve is the next best thing. He treats my brother as if he is his blood brother. There were times when my brother would request Mike's company and not mine. So many times, talks between the two of them about sports and the news were shared over cups of coffee. At times, there would be the phone call in the middle of the night from my brother. It prompted my husband to jump out of bed and go comfort him because my brother may have had a bad dream. I would get a kiss goodbye from Mike, and he'd be on his way. I hoped he wouldn't hit his angel wings as he ran out the door.

Mike decorates for the holidays by making many trips back and forth from my brother's locker where many treasures were stored. Mike sits through hospital visits and doctor visits asking questions and looking for answers so he can take the best care of my brother. Mike worked with him at physical therapy constantly thinking of ways to help him reach his goals. He did a lot of land and swimming therapy with him. He takes care of the van and always makes sure it is in working order. He works in the garden in the heat, cold, and rain. He would do anything that would make Father Steve's life easier and happier. Mike will make numerous calls to the wheelchair company whenever my brother's chair isn't working properly. Mike served at Mass every Saturday for years until COVID-19 surfaced. He always made sure my brother had enough to eat and would think nothing of stopping what he was doing and picking up some supper for him. He drove sixteen months every day to get back and forth to Cleveland to check on Father Steve and his progress. Summers weren't bad, but the two words *Cleveland* and *winter* can turn into a nightmare. There were times when we would follow the lights of the truck in front of us because we couldn't even see where the road ended because there was so much snow. We always made it home safely, showered, went to sleep, and started on our journey the next morning.

Mike and I have always been close, but all this time together has brought us closer. In June of 2023 we will celebrate our forty-fifth wedding anniversary. He isn't only my husband and my best friend, but now I know that he is my guardian angel too!

FAITH TO FRIENDS

Give thanks to the Lord, for he is good,
his mercy endures forever.
—Psalm 118:1 (NABRE)

Father Steve's life often revolves around six words beginning with the letter *F*. The six words that pretty much fill his day are: *faith, family, fishing, food, football,* and *friends*. These words come in a different order daily—except of course, his number one pick of the day, which always is *faith*.

A faith-filled day might consist of Mass, a prayer service, blessing one of the patients at his facility, watching the movie *The Chosen*, or maybe simply praying quietly in his room. All in all, each form of prayer is special.

Father Steve's family consists of four siblings that join him for Mass, prayer services, and may even take a ride in his van with him to other various churches where he has and does participate in the ceremonies. Sometimes just a fun ride on a beautiful day is just what he needs. We continually support him and his ministry. For him, the words *family* and *friends* definitely go together. We keep in touch with each other and constantly check on each other. We are all very interconnected with each other, even though some of us live many miles away. Even though Mike and Father Steve are not related by blood you would never know the difference. Many times, Mike just calls him brother. Mike truly belongs in this category too.

The word *fishing* and the Popovich family go hand in hand. Fishing is a sport that is loved by Father Steve, whether he fished as a child or continues to go fishing now. Fishing takes him into a relaxing environment which he often needs.

The word *food* for my brother is delivered in many different forms by family and friends. Some food is delivered by local restaurants, some comes in takeout containers, and some homemade food comes wrapped in warm dishes ready to be eaten. A special thank-you to all of you who have brought delicious meals to my brother. Some days are healthy food days, and others are grazing snack days. We all love and need those days too.

Father Steve loves the word *football* and a good football game whether high school, college, or pro. He had gone to many football games prior to his accident. Now, he spends time watching football on tv because the cold weather here is not a desirable environment for him.

Father Steve has many friends that can fall under the family category. I compare them to the 7-Eleven gas station. This gas station is open for business twenty-four hours, seven days a week. His friends are just like that. Just like the gas station, they are there for him twenty-four hours a day and seven days a week. You can call on them at any moment, and they will stop what they are doing if my brother needs something.

FAITH

> Therefore, since we have been justified by faith, we have peace with God through our Lord Jesus Christ, through whom we have gained access [by faith] to this grace in which we stand, and we boast in hope of the glory of God.
> —Romans 5:1–2 (NABRE)

The definition of faith is having complete trust or confidence and assurance in someone or something. Faith is unquestionable proof that doesn't require proof or evidence.

Faith is a word that has a special meaning to everyone, and many people have different thoughts about what the word means to them. To some people, it may mean dedicating their whole life to God like a priest or nun would. To others, faith is simply going to Mass on Sunday and being fairly nice to others during the week. I asked a few friends what their definition of *faith* is, and their answers varied. Some of their answers were that *faith* means "trust," "belief," "hope," "walking an unknown path," "belief without seeing," "comfort," "commitment," "their heart," "knowing that God is always there," "believing without question," "warmth," and lastly, *faith* was defined as "the man who runs the soup kitchen."

Having faith in Jesus Christ means relying completely on him. It means trusting in his infinite power, wisdom, and love. It includes believing in his teachings even though it may be hard for one to understand all that he does. Hopefully, we don't take our faith and all our rituals for granted. Our faith, like the kingdom of heaven, is a treasure. Let us never forget that!

Martin Luther King Jr. tells us that "faith is taking the first step even when you don't see the whole staircase. Faith is about believing that things will work out in the end."

The song "We Walk by Faith" by Marty Hogan, is a beautiful religious song that reminds us that we don't need to see things for us to believe in them.

They say that faith can move mountains. Now, that sounds like a big and important word to me. I have a strong faith, and now that I look back at my life, faith has moved mountains for me in the last ten years. Sometimes, watching my brother struggle and trying to say and do the right thing for him is like moving my own mountain.

The word *Faith* is tattooed on my left wrist with the letter *S* behind it. The letter *S*, of course, stands for my brother Father Steve. On my right wrist, I have a tattoo of a cross. When I think I'm having a bad day, I put my left hand under my right wrist and my right hand over my left wrist, wait a little while, then realize my little problem or struggle is not nearly as bad as what my brother is dealing with. I need to take a deep breath, say a prayer and move on. I quickly focus on what's really going on and quickly realize my problem is trivial compared to the problems of many others.

Charles and Pauline Popovich, our parents.

FAMILY

Children obey your parents for this is right. "Honor your father and mother." This is the first commandment with a promise, "that it may go well with you and that you may have a long life on earth." Fathers, do not provoke your children to anger, but bring them up with the training and instruction of the Lord.
—Ephesians 6:1–4 (NABRE)

Many people have beautiful definitions about the word *family* including the Bible. Michael J. Fox tells us that, "Family is not an important thing. It is everything." George Santayana tells us that, "The family is one of nature's masterpieces."

Family means having someone to love you unconditionally despite you and your shortcomings. They see the best in you when you can't see it and are there to continually offer each other support.

In 1979, a number one song was written and produced by Nile Rodgers and Bernard Edwards. It was titled "We Are Family." This song tells of the sisterhood of three girls. My baby sister was born when I was nineteen years old, so I basically grew up with three brothers. Ironically, I was blessed with three sons, so I've been surrounded by males a good part of my life. It's a beautiful thing though, because they spoil me and always take care of me, making me feel special.

My life is like this song except I belong to the brotherhood with one other female and me. The lyrics of the song tell us what life is like when you are close to your siblings.

My life began on June 6, 1953. I grew up with three brothers, Charlie, John, and Steve. Charlie is one year older than me and Father Steve is one year younger. John is seven years younger than me. Growing up at the 540 Miller Street residence was wonderful.

Elizabeth came along when I was nineteen years old and a welcomed surprise. My mom had her when she was forty-two years old. Elizabeth and I shared a room together, and although we no longer share that room together, we share many things together. She was the flower girl in my wedding, and even though we are nineteen years apart, you would never know that. She went from flower girl to best friend, along with my other siblings and Mike. When the two of us get together it's always a fun time and there's always a lot of hugs. It might be lunch at a restaurant, a spa day, or some shopping, but no matter what, there is a lot of laughter. As I am typing this story, my sister and I are texting, always keeping in touch. There's a lot of "he-he" and "ha-ha" going on in the text. Once again, laughing. We have a great bond! Our families often vacation together too, so now the whole family gets together for a fun fest.

In some ways, Elizabeth and I are very different. I'm a "maximalist," and I love to be surrounded by my "stuff." She is a "minimalist," and she likes to be surrounded by "space." She's the "smart" one, and I'm the "creative" one. Even though we are different, we are much alike when it comes to what's important to our brother.

We went to Saint Mathias school and Cardinal Mooney high school. My dad worked hard to pay for our education because a Catholic education was all he wanted for us. We were Sunday Mass churchgoers and never missed the Stations of the Cross during Lent.

We did a lot of outside activities and lived in a neighborhood full of kids. Every night we played badminton, baseball, hide-and-seek, and my favorite, ghost in the graveyard. Our neighbors were all okay with us running through the yards and back then it was safe to be outside late at night. We spent a lot of time at the local swimming pool called Pemberton pool or Shady Run swimming pool where we learned to swim. We had a beautiful amusement park called Idora Park located very close to our home that we frequented often. Seeing that park burn down years later was one sad sight. We spent winters sled riding and ice skating on the lake where we sometimes fished in the summer.

My mom, Pauline, was the rock of the family, and by her example, she showed me how to take care of my husband, house, children, and grandchildren. She was a very faith-filled woman and showed me by her example how I could become one too. I wanted to grow up just like her! She had a love for the Blessed Virgin, and you wouldn't dare call her during the time when she watched the rosary on TV.

She taught me how to sew and made me my first Holy Communion dress. She also spent many hours at the sewing machine making Barbie doll clothes for me. To this day, sixty-plus years later, I still have those Barbie outfits that my granddaughters play with now. My mom had a beautiful little sewing box, organized and pretty for all her sewing projects. She also had a box packed for life. It was filled with patience, generosity, creativity, dedication, compassion, and love of family and God. She not only had a talent for sewing, but also for music. She loved to play the harmonica and did a great job at it as she did with drawing.

She was a great cook and baker and loved spending time with her grandchildren. Whether she served them her special dish called "hamburger in the oven" or soup and a simple grilled cheese sandwich, she treasured her time with them.

I learned a very good lesson from my mom. Whenever she was upset, she stayed quiet and had nothing to say. While using this valuable lesson, I never have to apologize and take words back that I say when I am angry or upset. I know that I can never take words back, so this keeps me from using them. Nothing good can come out of an angry mouth. I like the quote, "If you don't have anything nice to say, then don't say anything at all." I used the same concept when I raised my children.

I watched my mom plant flowers and vegetables and learned a lot from her gardening lessons that I use to this very day. I am sure she is very proud of my flower gardens and Father Steve's gardens. I inherited her "love of planting" gene. My sons seem to have inherited this gene also. They are excited about gardening, and their grandmother would be proud of their flower and vegetable gardens as much as I am.

My dad, Charles, known to many as *Chap,* was a quiet man, but a man who loved to have fun. He was a hard worker, working in the steel mills his entire married life. He loved to go polka dancing with my mom. I'm sure that my parents are doing a lot of that in heaven.

He was also a faith-filled parent. My favorite memory of him is at night when he would kneel by the side of the bed and say his prayers. If I stayed up later than him, I could sit on the couch, and I could see into his room and watch him kneel there and pray. Father Steve told me that when he went to the garden of Gethsemane in the Holy Land, he pictured our Lord kneeling down and praying. He said he immediately pictured our dad kneeling at his bedside praying. I wanted to grow up just like him, loving God so much. My father loved the season of Lent, and it is ironic that my dad's birthday was April 3, the day that it is recorded that Jesus died. My dad was also able to celebrate his last birthday in 1993 during Lent, just five days after Ash Wednesday.

My father had a love for fishing and always went fishing with his brothers. They took really good care of him in the boat because he could not swim. He was always proud of the fish he caught, and at times, he brought them home, and I would watch him clean them in the basement. I inherited his "love for fishing" gene, and I still love to go fishing to this day. My dad's tackle box was clean and organized just like my mom's sewing box, and he too had a box packed for life.

He filled it with dedication, generosity, honesty, loyalty, fun and love of family and God.

My dad also loved his grandchildren very much. When they were little, he would crawl around on the floor pretending to be a dog. We nicknamed him Brownie. That name stuck with him, and I often found myself calling him Brownie instead of Dad up to the day he passed away. He is probably so excited as he is watching from heaven seeing that they've all inherited his "love of fishing" gene too. His grandsons are passing on this gene to their children also.

My dad and mom had a rock-solid marriage before passing away respectfully, March 1, 1993, and August 7, 2011. The Bible tells us in Ecclesiastes that, yes, there is a season for everything, but there never seems to be the right season or day for death.

Ironically, my house number came to haunt me later in life. I pulled up to the nursing facility for a visit, where my mom lived and looked at the clock in her car. It was 5:40 p.m. I immediately had a terrible feeling in my gut. I went to her room and said hello, and immediately sat down to read the newspaper because she looked so peaceful that I didn't want to bother her. In my head, I realized what that peaceful look meant. She was no longer with us. Why couldn't she have waited just a little longer until I got there to say goodbye? She knew that I was on my way. Why couldn't I get one last hug? I wanted just a little bit more of her wisdom about faith and life. Maybe she realized that I had already gotten fifty-eight years of her good example and that would be enough. I guess she knew goodbye would be way too hard for me. My mom probably just didn't want to break my heart, but a piece of my heart went along with her on August 7, 2011. The once happy 540 house number now had a very sad meaning. It was then recorded that 5:40 p.m. was the time of her death. She peacefully lay there, body in bed, but her soul in heaven. It was time to make phone calls and arrangements. Father Steve had the strength of Samson in the Bible to make it through her funeral Mass and homily. It was a warm sunny day in August just like the disposition of my mom. It was beautiful!

A few days later, the weather stayed bright and sunny. My family all met at Saint Paul's church, where Father Steve was the pastor, and we were all strategically sitting around the lake where we thought we would catch "the big one." We did catch quite a few fish, but nothing to brag about. As my dad watched looking down from heaven with my mom, it must have been a beautiful sight to see all of us placed around the lake and doing what we learned best from him—fishing. We all miss our parents very much, but we continue living with the family values that they taught us. We all keep faith, the number one priority in our lives. We all take care of each other even though the whole family is not living together in the same state.

I wasn't there on the day that my dad passed away either. I guess neither one of them liked goodbyes. Once again, I didn't get that last hug. At least my mom was with him at home, so she must have gotten it and that was perfect. I guess my dad didn't want to break my heart. Once again, a piece of my heart went to heaven, this time with my dad on March 1, 1993. I was at home taking care of my three sons, exactly where he would have wanted me to be. Once again phone calls and plans were made. The weather was cold on the day we buried my dad in March. Snow was not predicted, but nothing could stop it on that day. The snow made a sad situation look beautiful. We made a snowman on the lawn in front of our porch of the house where we lived for so many years and spent so many family gatherings. After the funeral luncheon, my family and I went to Mill Creek Park, and we all went sled riding. My dad would have wanted us to have fun together and celebrate his life by spending time with each other. We piled up on sleds, and I can't remember who was on the bottom, but they ended up with bruised ribs. It was a good time for all. I guess that was easy for me to say because I wasn't the one at the bottom with three people on top of me. When we were finished, we looked around and found a beautiful snow-blanketed area. There was not one footprint in there. It was the perfect place to make snow angels for our father. We lay in the snow with our arms and legs moving and waited there until someone could pick us up so that we wouldn't mess up the angel. When we were done, we looked at our masterpiece. There were probably ten snow angels looking up to heaven at our father and mother. A sight I'll never forget!

FISHING

After he had finished speaking, he said to Simon, "Put out into deep water and lower your nets for a catch." Simon said in reply, "Master we have worked hard all night and have caught nothing, but at your command I will lower the nets." When they had done this, they caught a great number of fish and their nets were tearing.
—Luke 5:4–6 (NABRE)

"Who will catch the big one?" is the question of the day for every fisherman. Well, that's if you're a true fisherman. The type or color really doesn't matter at all. The weight and size are the two important features.

While growing up, my family would start our Sunday with morning Mass and then pack what we would need for the day at Lake Arrowhead. My mom and I would pack sunglasses, a blanket, a cooler and a picnic basket. The cooler and picnic basket were filled with drinks, sandwiches, and lots of snacks and goodies. We almost couldn't wait to get there just to eat. The food that we would pick up on the way home would be just as exciting.

My dad would pack up the fishing poles and tackle box. The tackle box contained bobbers, string, leaders, hooks, sinkers, lures, extra fishing line, a stringer, and needle-nose pliers to remove hooks out of the fish. It was very organized, and my dad was proud of his tackle box. We stopped to buy bait on the way to the lake. We were ready and good to go. The word *fishing* now came into play.

It was always a fun Sunday. My siblings and I stood in a straight line and threw our bamboo poles into the water one at a time. We never took our eyes off the bobber in hopes of pulling in the biggest fish that swam in that lake. Competition in my family started way back then. We'd often get tangled up and my dad would put his high-tech Mitchell pole down, which we never touched, and patiently untangle the mess that we previously made. Most of the time, we caught bluegills or sunfish. I guess the fancy big fish were out in the middle of the lake, but we weren't quite ready to get in a boat. On the way home, my dad would stop and buy some fresh corn on the cob and watermelon, and we always stopped for ice cream. He would take the fish home to clean them, and we would have them for supper.

It wasn't important how many fish we caught, we just knew that Sunday afternoon never had a dull moment, and the family time was perfect and priceless! I would eventually learn how being "fishers of men" would tie into my brother's past. "Fishers of men" is a phrase that is used in the Gospel. Jesus told his first disciples, Simon Peter and Andrew, who cast their nets into the Sea of Galilee to become "fishers of men." They were just simple men in a simple boat who had no high-tech equipment to catch fish. "Fishers of men" means to win people for Christ. You are a "soul winner." Sometimes you win over new people who are just learning about Jesus and sometimes you can bring back people to the Catholic faith who have left. Either way, you are a "fisher of men." You can also be any age to be a "fisher of men." Just as Father Steve will try to catch fish at the lake, he continuously plants his hook into people, and he constantly introduces them to God or maybe even brings them back to the church if they have strayed.

Little did I know that the six-year-old that I fished next to would become a true "fisher of men." Now that I look back, there was a true meaning to my brother's life sixty-plus years ago.

We never matched the story of Jesus and the miracle of the fish. He fed five thousand people with two fish and five loaves of bread. We were always content with enough fish to make us a nice and tasty supper, but what a sight it would have been to see what Jesus could have done with our few fish.

To this very day, my brother loves to go to his most recent parish, St. Paul's, where that beautiful lake sits in front of the rectory. He often gets frustrated trying to fish and often gets tangled in the string. The hook usually gets caught in his clothes and at some point, he'll end up throwing the pole down. He now decides that he would just rather sit under the cool shade of a tree, relax, and watch everyone else fish. He always tells me there's a "big one" in the lake somewhere, and he always encourages us to catch it. I'm not sure what I would do if I caught the big one, but I'm sure it would put a smile on my brother's face. It's always a nice memory and a fun day to go to St. Paul's and fish.

Every now and then I take a ride to Lake Arrowhead with my husband, Mike, and look over to the lake and picture where the famous picnic bench sat where my family placed our blanket and fished so many years ago and so many times. It always brings back the happiest of memories. Condominiums now circle the lake, so it is no longer open to the public. I would sure love to take my grandchildren there who all love to fish and show them what once was their grandma's favorite fishing spot.

In 2015, while my while my brother was in rehab, he was in the activity room and painted a picture for me. It's a picture of a boat sitting in the sand next to water. One of the activity aides made some footprints in the sand to help depict Father's choice of his "Footprints in the Sand" painting. We need to remember that we are carried by God during the hard times in our life, and I believe that we all are probably quite the load for him until we can finally stand alone.

FOOD

For I was hungry and you gave me food, I was thirsty and
you gave me drink, a stranger and you welcomed me.
—Matthew 25:35 (NABRE)

Food is one of the *F* words that Father Steve enjoys, especially when he has a good appetite.

He was a true foodie before his accident and loved to eat. He knew the best restaurants to eat at and he enjoyed going out with his family, friends, or even sitting with some perfect strangers.

Father's favorites were always the meals that our mom made. Her homemade meals were the best! Father Steve loved my mom's potato pancakes. To this day, if I tell him that I am bringing him some potato pancakes, he will have his fork in his hand waiting until I get there. When I first made her Easter bread recipe—of course, you can't celebrate Easter without it—I put a framed picture of her on the table to watch me. I looked at her and asked her for some guidance. She sure was there with me because my Easter bread was a success. I went outside, looked up to heaven, and I knew that she was looking down at me giving me a thumbs up.

I try to duplicate some of her recipes but haven't mastered any of them yet. This Easter, I made another attempt at the Easter bread with my eldest son, Mikey. It was a true success, and I'm sure my mom was smiling down at us. My siblings and sons are pretty good at trying to match her recipes. I only wish I would have paid more attention to her cooking when I was at home growing up, but I was somehow busy living my silly teenage life.

Right after the accident, my brother was not permitted to eat or drink anything. He was so disappointed when his eating came to a halt. He had to pass something called a "swallow test" before his medical team would even let him flirt with the idea of eating any food. In order to pass the test, he needed the ability to drink an entire amount of required liquid continuously. He also could not cough up to one minute after the swallowing attempt, and there could not be the beginning of a wet, gurgly or horse vocal quality. If any of these signs were present, it meant that he would not have passed the test. After three attempts and three weeks of not passing the test, my brother finally passed his challenge of the swallow test. I used to stand by the door so I could listen to what the technician said to him. I needed to prepare myself so that when he wheeled himself out of the room, I was ready to process his excitement or disappointment.

After he passed his test, the first thing that he requested to eat was a bowl of Rice Krispies. We rushed to the store looking for the box showcasing the cartoon characters, Snap, Crackle, and Pop. I'm sure at this point he didn't even care if he heard any snap, crackle, or pop. He just wanted to eat. With spoon in hand and a smile on his face, he tackled the bowl of cereal. He said it felt like he was eating at a buffet, and he was so celebrative about it. His speech pathologist was so excited for him that she went home, made him some macaroni and cheese and brought it to work. Who can turn down home-made macaroni and cheese? It's such a comfort food, especially when you're not well. My brother's third request was a hot dog, an all-American icon. Now that's the easiest food to choke on, so he had to be very careful when he was eating it. Little by little, he was permitted to add new foods to his diet. It was finally time that we could eat in front of him too. We never wanted to eat or drink in front of him when he wasn't allowed to do the same. We didn't even have coffee because he loved the beverage, and the smell of it would disappoint a man who was not permitted to drink it. We were all so glad that those days were behind us.

Food is a staple that Father Steve needs to keep him healthy. On some days he is blessed with a super appetite, and on other days, he is not feeling well and doesn't have any desire to eat. The smell of food, unfortunately, makes it so he can't even entertain the thought of eating. A great friend of his, who previously owned a restaurant, has been there for the last ten years serving him delicious meals that were also nutritious. While in the hospital, my brother would call his friend on the spur of the moment, and he'd bring any meal that my brother desired. If he didn't have time to bring it up, he would find somebody that would deliver it. This helped my brother to maintain good health. He has been serving my brother delicious meals for the last twenty-plus years that he has known my brother. They met while my brother resided at a parish and this friend's restaurant was within walking distance to my brother's parish rectory. How lucky was he? Talk about a great friend! Another good friend makes sure that her nut rolls get delivered to Father Steve during the Christmas season. Healthy food is great, but everyone deserves a yummy dessert every now and then. His special friends surprise him from time to time with their delicious home-cooked meals. A local restaurant often delivers pizza to him with just a quick phone call. His family will bring up some home-cooked meals consisting of foods that he grew up eating. I think his favorite choice right now would be potato pancakes, a steak dinner with a baked potato, or some kind of pasta with a tasty meatball. We really try to push him to eat protein because it is such an important part of a healthy diet. It helps build and repair muscles and can be used as an energy source. It's also good to help maintain skin elasticity which is important because his skin needs to stay healthy to prevent wounds.

I love it when my brother calls and says that he wants to eat. It's music to my ears!

FOOTBALL

> To satisfy the one recruited him, a soldier does not
> become entangled in the business affairs of life.
> Similarly, an athlete cannot receive the winner's crown
> except by competing according to the rules.
> —2 Timothy 2:4–5 (NABRE)

The word *football* simply brings a smile to my brother's face. Cardinal Mooney High School in Youngstown, Ohio, was Father Steve's alma mater. He also worked there as the assistant principal, so he really supports the school and team. He followed the team wherever they traveled, even to the playoffs. He went to many Mooney football games before his accident but hasn't been to any since his injury. Often, when Cardinal Mooney played against its biggest cross-town Catholic high school rival, my brother could not attend the games because of the suspense of what the outcome would be.

Youngstown State University, YSU, was also Father Steve's alma mater. He graduated magna cum laude in 1977 with a bachelor of arts degree. He became very passionate about YSU football, especially with the hiring of Coach Jim Tressel. In the early 1990s, Jim Tressel was able to take the team to ten playoff games. They also won four National Championships out of the ten years. The YSU stadium, commonly known by fans as the Ice Castle, is a beautiful stadium. It got its nickname from the freezing cold nights that a football game in Northeast, Ohio, has to offer. At one time, it was unique as it only had seating on one side. Father loved going to these YSU games and often tailgated before the game. Always a good time!

Father Steve and his great friend, Father Ed Noga, decided to go to a YSU football game that would be held in Chattanooga,

Tennessee. This football Championship game would be played at the Finley stadium between the YSU Penguins and the Georgia Southern Eagles. The event took place on December 18, 1999. Since Father Steve and Father Noga were such avid followers of the YSU football team, they decided to have a banner made which read "Priests for Penguins." The penguin is the YSU mascot. While in Chattanooga, Father Steve and Father Noga decided they would hang their banner outside of the window of their motel room. Once they went outside and started to hang the banner, the window closed behind them locking them outside. As they were calling down for people to help them, people saw the banner and just started clapping for them, yelling, "Go Penguins." The people did not realize that the two priests were locked outside and were calling to them for assistance. After being locked outside for a short while, someone from the hotel staff realized that two people were where they shouldn't be, so they came up, opened the door to their room and rescued them from being locked outside. Unfortunately, the two priests did not bring success to the game as YSU lost to Georgia Southern, but they sure rooted for the team and showed their support.

Father Steve is also an avid Pittsburgh Steelers fan. Our father worked in the steel mills his whole life. Father Steve says that he loved the named Steelers because it had the word *steel* in it, and he loved his father, so he became a fan. He was able to go to a few Pittsburgh Steeler games. He said a player that stands out to him is Franco Harris, a football running back. He was known for being a gentleman, a classy kind of guy. He has given Pittsburgh fans numerous memories not only from the football field, but he has also given back and improved the Pittsburgh community through his business and generous contributions.

FRIENDS

> Faithful friends are a sturdy shelter; whoever finds one finds a treasure. Faithful friends are beyond price, no amount can balance their worth. Faithful friends are lifesaving medicine; those who fear God will find them.
> —Wisdom of Ben Sira 6:14–16 (NABRE)

Friend is a word that can be described as a person who has a strong liking for and trust in one another. Friends are dependable, very loyal and empathetic. A beautiful quality of a friend is how they are nonjudgmental. A good friend will often provide emotional support, have a positive effect on your life, and you will enjoy spending time with them. They have your back no matter what. A good friend will watch out for you, make sure you're safe, feel supported, and make you feel that you're loved. A good friend will never purposely lead you into making decisions or taking actions that aren't good for you. A good friend will stand by you no matter what decision you make, whether they agree or disagree.

Father's clergy friends are important to him because they complete his day, fulfilling his spiritual needs. His priestly friends keep in touch with him and invite him to their parishes to join in faith-filled services.

Father Ed Noga, who was the pastor at St. Patrick Church in Youngstown, Ohio, before his retirement, invited Father Steve to the parish to celebrate Mass with him many times. Father Steve joined in Holy Week services and performed a blessing of the sick at one service. People were teary-eyed because Father Steve sat in his wheelchair and blessed others for their various ailments almost as if he forgot about his own. The people from this parish truly support him and always invite him over for their parish spaghetti dinners. Many women of the parish baked beautiful desserts for Father Steve to use at a cake raffle booth during the fall fest at his current facility. The fall fest followed his polka Mass.

He has spoken at mission services at St. Edward's and St. Paul's Churches. He has baptized babies at St. Brendan's church, and one of the baptisms at Immaculate Heart of Mary Church was for his nephew Joey's baby girl, Alaina. He also participated in Holy Thursday services and washed the feet of parishioners just as Jesus washed the feet of his disciples. If the weather permits, he will show up at the distribution of food at Immaculate Heart of Mary parish food pantry and mingle with the workers providing support. He may even show up for a weightlifting contest to give the competitors support. This generous parish keeps in touch with him constantly after he spent fifteen years as their pastor. They will always help Father Steve with anything that he needs.

He also very much enjoys going to St. Robert's Church in Cortland, Ohio, where he would join his friend, Father Carl Kish, to concelebrate Mass. It is a very welcoming and wonderful parish. Father Steve never even felt like he had a disability when he was there because everyone made him feel like he fit right in, like a missing piece in a puzzle. They would also invite him, his nurse and his family to their parish picnic. His priest friends have stuck together and have supported him.

Father Steve has a very eclectic group of friends. He has been so blessed with the best of the best! His friends have an interpersonal bond with him. They're around 24-7 and help to meet all his needs. Some have been friends for a very long time. One great friend has paid for the daily newspaper for Father Steve for many years. If you know him, you know how much he loves his morning coffee and morning newspaper. Some are friends from different parishes where he was a pastor. Some are friends that he met along the way. His friends have passed along many good books to read. They might stop with the book in one hand and a pizza in the other. They may come for a short visit just to chat a bit or maybe a quiet visit when Father

Steve wants silence, but a friend within his sight. Sometimes quiet company is the best company!

Father Steve was having a tough day when one of his friends came to visit. He talked to my brother and asked why the room looked so dark and gloomy. He immediately turned on some lights and pulled up the shade. He told my brother that he would come back every day and do the same thing if he kept the room dark. Needless to say, the lights are usually on now unless he is sleeping. Now that's a good friend!

Father Steve's friends have helped with continued physical therapy. Some of his friends had even gone to swimming therapy with him and had spent hours in the pool encouraging him to push as hard as he could. They helped get him in and out of the pool with constant cautiousness about how my brother was handled to avoid any skin issues. There were days when he did not want a cheerleader in the pool with him, and if you were a good friend, you would know when to be vocal and when to be silent.

Friends will watch sporting events on TV with him too. Food is usually involved when a good football or basketball game comes on. Most of them have been friends for a very long time. A lot of his friends are simply like family!

FATHER STEVE

> My son, do not forget my teaching, take to heart my commands;
> For many days, and years of life, and peace, will they bring you.
> —Proverbs 3:1–2 (NABRE)

Father Steve was born on Wednesday, November 24, 1954. His zodiac sign is the Sagittarius. People born under this sign usually attract others to them, and they project an aura of youth and charm.

They are very optimistic, extroverts, loyal, smart, assertive, compassionate, and one-of-a-kind. All these attributes truly define Father Steve. Although as a child he was a quiet little boy, he grew up to be a fun and boisterous man with the physique of a weightlifter. I don't really follow astrology; however, things seem to fit in place with Father Steve and his birthdate. The astrological element of the sign Sagittarius is fire. This may account for his love of a hot smoking grill with briquets on fire and fireworks in the sky. The life path number of a person born on November 24, 1954, is number nine. This is quite ironic because a cat has nine lives, and my brother has often been described as a cat who has nine lives since he has made it through so many illnesses and surgeries. The ironic part is my brother is allergic to cats. His birthdate zodiac animal is the horse. The horse represents the spiritual power of independence, freedom, confidence, nobleness, and endurance. Its' symbol is associated with strength, courage, and freedom. All these qualities and values really do describe Father Steve, so maybe there is something to my brother and his birth date.

He grew up going to Saint Mathias grade school where he was a server and a lector. As a child he enjoyed fishing, baseball, and delivering the newspaper. It was fun on Saturdays to go with him house to house and collect money for the *Vindicator*, our local newspaper. People were often home and had their money set aside for payment. They waited for us to come. We often got great tips and some hot cookies for the road. Hot chocolate was offered to us on cold days, and in Northeast Ohio we had many cold and snowy days. Also, he was the janitor at the school, loved that job, and loved the church. Musically inclined, he enjoyed playing the guitar.

After graduating from St. Matthias grade school, my brother's next step would be a Catholic high school, Cardinal Mooney where he would join his brother Charlie and sister Margie. We lived close to the school, so we were able to walk every day. He strived for excellence at high school where he was a member of the Latin and drama clubs. He starred in the *King and I*, before graduating in 1972.

Father Steve's next school adventure would be Youngstown State University where he would graduate Magna Cum Laude with a Bachelor of Arts degree. He then attended St. Mary's Seminary in Cincinnati, Ohio. During those four years he reached the pinnacle of his theological studies. He earned a master's degree in Scripture from St. Mary's. While a seminarian, he served as scout chaplain at Camp Stambaugh. Due to his exemplary leadership, the Boy Scouts earned their Pius XII Award. During summer studies, Father earned a master's degree in religious education from Fordham University in the Bronx.

In 1980, Father Steve was ordained as a deacon. He interned as deacon at St. John's and at Saint Paul's located in Canton Ohio. On June 6, 1981, Father Steve was ordained as a priest at the Saint Columba Cathedral in Youngstown, Ohio, by Bishop James W Malone. St. Matthias church was the setting for his first Mass on June 7, 1981.

Father Steve's Ordination Day.

Proud parents on Ordination Day.

    In 1981, Father Steve served at Saint James Parish in Warren as an associate. At that time, he became chaplain of the Catholic Boy Scouts of Trumbull County. He then taught at Saint Thomas Aquinas High School in Louisville, Ohio, from 1984 through 1989 and served as chaplain of the Catholic Committee on Scouting in Stark County. In 1989, Father Steve became associate principal at his alma mater, Cardinal Mooney High School, in Youngstown. While at Cardinal Mooney, he was chaplain of the football team. In July 1992, he became pastor of Saint Lucy Parish in Campbell, Ohio. It didn't take long at all for an Italian parish to love this Slovak priest who pulled up to their church on a motorcycle. St. Lucy's was known for their delicious spaghetti dinners and bake sales. Needless to say, my brother ate very well while residing at this parish. Our whole family ate well also. When there was a spaghetti dinner, we were served not only a plate of spaghetti, but a large bowl of spaghetti was set in front of us for seconds. My children weren't given just a glass of pop; pitchers of pop sat right in front of their very eyes. Desserts came next. If you said that you were going to St. Lucy's for anything, my kids were in the car before me. They sponsored an indoor festival and decorated a house that they owned for Halloween, turning it into a haunted house. Father Steve was involved, of course, in this Halloween project because it would bring excitement and fun for the children. Being a kid at heart, he was always involved in activities that made children smile.

It is said that Father Steve made serving Mass not only special, but fun. When the servers had their annual getaway and went to Geauga Lake for the day, Father Steve not only went with them, but participated in all the fun activities by joining the kids on the waterslides. At Christmas, instead of just having a party for the Mass servers, he turned it into a family Christmas party and even had a sleigh with horses to pull the families on a sleigh ride and just as expected, it snowed that night!

Father Steve had a very close friend who was a coach, and my brother became the only team priest of a public school. He would share a prayer before and after every game. He resonated with the team since he was a weightlifter. Often, you would find him joining in basketball practice on a Saturday. He spent time not only playing basketball but talking and listening to what the high schoolers had to say. Sometimes, when they were presented with problems, they had no trouble sharing these problems with Father Steve because they gained his trust and wanted some direction in their life. He helped them in making better decisions to keep them off the streets. They learned to think of Father Steve before they made these decisions. Father Steve had team coaches play a big part in his life, so he wanted to do the same for these boys. After this team, the Campbell Memorial Red Devils won the state championship in Columbus, Ohio, Father Steve celebrated the Mass in the lobby of the hotel where they were staying. About fifty people gathered to join in this celebration, which took place the morning after the victory. No one at the hotel had a problem with what had taken place. Father Steve's coach friend describes Father Steve like this: "The title *priest* doesn't make him something special. He makes the title *priest* something special."

That same year, he was elected and served as representative to the Priests' Personnel Board. Father Steve joined the Knights of

Columbus, Salem Council 1818. In July 1992, he became cochaplain of Marian. Co. 3813, Campbell, Ohio. In 1993, Father Steve became the chaplain of the Greater Youngstown Area Chapter. And in 1994, he was honored at a banquet as chaplain of the year.

In 1994, he was appointed Director of Continuing Education for the Youngstown diocese. With this title, he planned and sought out speakers to attend the workshop for his fellow priests. He was in this position for fifteen years. He was able to plan workshops south of the Mason-Dixon Line, and in February when it is so cold in Northeast Ohio, this would be a nice little get away for the priests. Workshops were set up in New Mexico, Arizona, Colorado, Texas, New Orleans, and California.

Father Steve's next assignment in 1995, would be at Immaculate Heart of Mary Parish, in Austintown, Ohio. His work would last there for fifteen years. He was involved in the Steering Committee of the Austintown 20/20 program and was very excited about the plans and direction that it offered the community. He was also appointed as one of the Austintown Fire Department chaplains. While he resided at this parish, he was involved with the Ulster Project and volunteered at the soup kitchen. He was involved in the festivals and weightlifting contests at the festivals. Also, he was involved in the Bible school for a few years. He began the Men's Renewal, where men gathered for a weekend, praying, singing, eating, sleeping and renewing their faith in God. After the renewal, these men would sponsor the next renewal for a new group of men. It was an empowering weekend, new friends were made, and the love of God was shared. You took this experience with you for the rest of your life. He was also involved in the school and did a lot of activities with the children during their school day. He always showed up at the church picnic and made sure that everybody there had a good time. When it was time for him to move on, his next assignment would be at Saint Paul's Parish in New Middletown, Ohio.

In 2010, Father Steve began his ministry at Saint Paul's Parish in New Middletown, Ohio. Mike and I helped to move him into the parish. He let me decorate the parish with all his precious items and we decorated a wall with twenty-one crosses. We called it the "wall of crosses." Whenever he obtained a new cross, it was added to the wall. He joined in all the activities at the church, all the picnics, helped with making perogies, and attended all meetings of the parish community.

His homilies were always colorful, and he loved having props. During one homily, when he was preaching about Zacchaeus and the sycamore tree, he brought in a tree to be raffled off at the church. One lucky winner went home, planted that tree, and was reminded of the Zacchaeus story whenever they looked at it. Zacchaeus was known primarily for his faith in climbing a sycamore tree to see Jesus, and his generosity in giving half of all that he possessed to those in need.

He spent a lot of time fishing in the lake right in front of the parish rectory. A lot of times he would sit there and prepare his weekend homily in his head that he would present at Mass. He was involved in the South Range parade, throwing a huge amount of candy to the children standing on the curbs. He worked at the prison ministry while he was at this parish. His work as this parish would suddenly come to a halt at about 9:00 a.m. on November 13, 2013.

Father Steve was always blessed with spectacular secretaries at his parishes. They were not only very professional employees, but friends. They looked out for him constantly and made sure he had everything that he needed for his ministry. They became close to all of us, and I always knew that my brother was in great hands when he was at the rectory. Thanks to all of you!

As you can see, Father Steve's life was busy and very productive. Before the accident, his life was filled with adventure and was unpredictable. He enjoyed the spontaneity of the day and lived his life to the fullest. You always heard him before you saw him. He was a big guy with a loud voice and an outgoing personality. He was loved by his family, parish, and community.

He was a happy-go-lucky, free spirit kind of guy. He always put others before himself, especially his family. He would accept a challenge like the polar bear plunge and would never worry about the outcome. He lived in the moment and never worried about the future. He spent every day in prayer and was only a phone call away if you needed him. He counseled people, administered the sacraments to them, and was involved in the prison ministry. He loved to ride his motorcycle. He took care of his family, his parish, the prisoners he ministered to, and oftentimes the community. He was involved in various community activities and even participated in parades and festivals. He was an adventuresome individual who loved a challenge. No adventure was too big for him, and he was quite the daredevil. He was a spur-of-the-moment kind of guy and last-minute planner. He was so busy with this ministry, and it was hard to make plans, but when a free moment popped up, he would call my house to see which one of my sons was available to go out and have a good time with him. Maybe it was for ice cream, or maybe to attend a basketball or football game. It didn't matter where you would go, you just knew that you would have the best time ever. I can only wonder what the future would have been for him if the accident hadn't happened. I guess we'll never know.

After the accident, his new life began. But he still lives a life that continues with the love of his family and old friends. It has also become enriched with some new friends, and a new and enhanced love of his faith and Jesus.

FATHER STEVE AND HIS SIBLINGS

While he was still speaking to the crowds, his mother and his brothers appeared outside, wishing to speak with him. [Someone told him, "Your mother and your brothers are standing outside, asking to speak with you."] But he said in reply to the one who told him, "Who is my mother? Who are my brothers?" And stretching out his hands toward his disciples, he said, "Here are my mother and my brothers. For whoever does the will of my heavenly Father is my brother, and sister, and mother."
—Matthew 12:46–50 (NABRE)

Father Steve has four siblings, consisting of two brothers and two sisters. Charlie lives in Pennsylvania and John lives in California. Elizabeth and I both live in Ohio.

Charlie is the oldest of the siblings. He is an individual that is hard to describe, and I think the terms *free spirit* or *free bird* would be the best title for him. He traveled many years working at his job, so I think that's how he kind of gets the "free spirit" title. He has a clever sense of humor and can make you laugh at a spur of the moment. In my brother Father Steve's eyes, Charlie is an enigma. Yes, I guess you can say he is almost larger than life. Since he traveled so much throughout his life we never know when Charlie was going to appear. Every time there was a holiday or party, we all had to wait for Charlie because his job took up a lot of his time with traveling. When Charlie showed up it was a huge deal. We were so excited to see him. To this day, Father Steve still has the excitement in his eyes when you mention Charlie's name. We still never know when Charlie's going to arrive. If I'm in the room and Charlie appears I'll soon turn into the little fly on the wall because guess what, Charlie's here! He's great medicine for Father Steve, and that's all that counts. Everybody needs a larger-than-life person in their life! And so do I!

Then, there's me, Margie. I am very easy to please and like the simple things in life, so I work at keeping Father's Steve's life as simple as can be. I spend a lot of time with him as you may notice in this book, and it is time well spent and I wouldn't have it any other way.

John lives in California so visiting Father Steve was not an easy task because of the distance and the demanding job that he has. When he can come, his visits are truly looked forward to by his brother and all of us. Since John cannot travel to Ohio often, most of his and Father Steve's communication is through phone calls.

Elizabeth is eighteen years younger than Father Steve. As I mentioned before, she's the "smart" one and I'm the "creative" one so when we get together with Father Steve, we cover all the bases of what he needs. He loves her company because she's bright, spirited and young. The advice I give to him is more like something an older person would say. The advice she gives to him is completely different because of her age and he needs this young advice. It's really good for him! He really looks forward to her visits because she has a whole different spin on life. She can take him to places in his mind that I can never reach. Her gifts to him are always quite unique too. They are never bought on the spur of the moment. They're very much thought out with his best interest in mind. I'm sure he toasts every cup of coffee to her because of her purchase of his Keurig coffee maker for him. He does love his cup of coffee like he does love his sister Elizabeth!

Father Steve's accident has affected me and my siblings in very different ways. I could not speak for them or explain how their experience of this accident was either the same or different from mine, so I asked them each to write a short story. The following three stories are from Charlie, John, and Elizabeth, written by them and in their own words.

Father Steve and brother, Charlie.

CHARLIE

> A good name is more desirable than great riches,
> and high esteem, than gold and silver.
> —Proverbs 22:1 (NABRE)

Since I was a railroad supervisor, I traveled the country and was away from family for at least twenty years. In those years, I missed many parties, weddings, birthdays, and much more. I was lucky though, because my family would relate different events or shenanigans that occurred during my absence to keep me in the loop. However, as I began to write my thoughts about my brother Father Steve, I realized that there are many things I did not know about the quiet strength, courage, and perseverance he possessed. The weekend fishing trips at Saint Paul's church in New Middletown, Ohio, was something I always looked forward to. We bought so much bait at the hardware store, they said, that we must be feeding the fish instead of catching them. Little did they know, we caught many fish and turtles too and with the amount of nightcrawlers we used, the fish were eating well. One day, I was caught off guard when the fish got hooked and dragged my fishing pole into the water, never to be seen again! We had many calamities during these weekend fishing expeditions. One day, I remember we sat for several hours, and it appeared the fish must have left the area. We did not even get a nibble. Father Steve always had a rational explanation when things were not going well. He simply stated, "The fish are much smarter than us!" I quickly responded, "Speak for yourself as I pulled up a huge bass." I loved the banter between us because he has a sense of humor and can pull off just about anything, while keeping a poker face intact. I always enjoyed my time with my brother, and I looked forward to the restaurant trips after fishing. We would talk, laugh, joke, and try to guess what people did for a living as we looked around at the other patrons. One thing for sure, my brother loved people and his love of people, along with his personality, were good characteristics for his role as Father Steve!

 I will never forget the day I was notified about his car crash, on November 13, 2013. He was on his way to celebrate Mass at the maximum-security prison, but unfortunately, he hit black ice and lost control of the vehicle, struck by a truck and then spun around in his car and struck a tree. The impact was so severe that when Father Steve was found in the car by the policer officer, he was unresponsive. The injuries sustained would have killed most people, but Father Steve survived. Even in his weakened state he never lost faith in the Lord he serves. When I think back to his service to others before this accident, I realized Father Steve impacted many lives through his faith, knowledge, wisdom, and humor. This is why he not only is my brother, but my best friend. When I think about all he has endured after this accident, it makes my daily challenges insignificant. Fortunately, his friends and family have stayed in touch and have always been grateful and feel that he has been blessed.

Father Steve and sister-in-law, Mary on election night.

When Mary met Father Steve

I invited Mary, who is now my wife, to Ohio to meet my parents and family on Mother's Day 1982. She was nervous, because she was a Protestant and my entire family was Catholic, with a brother, Father Steve, and uncle, Father George, as priests. I wanted to let them know we planned to be married but she was not sure how it was going to go. My family was great and treated her well, but complications arose about where the marriage would take place. To this day, I'm certain my brother Father Steve played a role in smoothing things out and on our wedding day we were married in the West Newton Presbyterian Church, by Reverend Day, Father George, and Father Steve. Mary often remarked how friendly and accepting my family was of her and her son Phil. We had a grand reception with over six hundred in attendance with a bar bill that could have been a down payment on a house. Mary fondly remembers the wonderful times at the Popovich homestead in Ohio, especially holidays when Father Steve would entertain the kids. Her son Phil just recently commented how much fun he had playing caroling bingo and all the other crazy games that Father Steve provided. My brother was very kind and generous to my new wife and her son, and my family always enjoyed participating in any event, especially if Father Steve was involved.

My wife decided to run for state representative in the Fifty-Eighth District in Pennsylvania in 2016. This was after Father Steve had recovered enough from his injuries to be placed in a long-term care facility, which would permit him to go out with family in his specialty van. Much to our surprise, guess who showed up to West Newton, Pennsylvania, in November, none other than Father Steve with his brother-in-law Mike Cretella as his designated driver. There was such a chill in the air, I wanted to stay home myself, but this goes to show you his moral character of perseverance.

Kindness often made my wife insist I take something homemade that Father Steve would enjoy. This included homemade coconut cream, blackberry pie, kolache or meatloaf, and vegetable soup. No matter what I brought, Father Steve always coaxed me to go out to one of his favorite restaurants, just like old times to enhance the delicious desserts. My wife stopped by several times to visit when she picked up perogies that Father Steve's previous parish sold for the annual sale in West Newton. It never failed that someone at the parish would inquire about Father's well-being. She always left with hugs, prayers, and good wishes for safe travels for her. This further demonstrates the effect Father Steve had on his congregation and anyone he met.

Joey Cretella

On a sunny cold day, Father Steve and I attended a Cardinal Mooney football game versus Ironton high school, which is nestled along the Ohio River. We decided to take our nephew Joey to the game, since his brothers, Mike and Tony, were to play in the band during this event. Joey was excited to spend a day with his uncles at a sporting event. As we neared the gate, we were overwhelmed by the crowd. The seating capacity of the stadium was ten thousand, and it appeared that most of the seats were filled. We enjoyed the game and at halftime we decided to get some fries and pizza, since we had worked up an appetite with our cheering and yelling during the game. The lines were long, and we decided to divide and conquer to get the food we wanted. I realize now that that was not a kid-smart decision. We told Joey, "Stay right here by the pizza stand. We will be back. Don't move a muscle. We will only be gone a few minutes." It seemed like we were only gone a few minutes, but most likely it was more than ten minutes. When we arrived back at the stand, Father Steve looked at me and I looked at him and we both said simultaneously, "Where's Joey?" "Margie is going to kill us!"

We searched frantically; the knots were welling up in my stomach. How are we going to explain that we lost Joey, her son, to my sister Margie? We had promised to look after him and I believe at the time he was only nine or ten years old. I knew Father Steve was worried also. He kept his cool, but we were running around calling his name, over a noisy crowd not realizing he would never hear us. What seemed like a lifetime, we spotted him near the pizza place, but he was so small and the wave of people standing in line, made him impossible to see. Of course, Father Steve assured me he was not worried and knew that we would find him. He went on to advise me that I should have settled for pizza instead of wanting french fries and this would have avoided the entire situation. I was so worked up about this event, I apologized to Father Steve. However, I now realize, my brother shifted the responsibility on me as a joke. He went with me to get the fries in the first place, so we are both at fault! In retrospect it is comical now, but thinking about the possibilities of what could have happened is not a laughing matter. I'm not sure if Joey remembers this day, but I can assure you that I won't ever forget the sinking feeling I had when I realized he was gone.

MARGIE CRETELLA

The Silver Mirror

My wife, Mary, and I were visiting my parents in Youngstown, Ohio, for Thanksgiving. After the activities and festivities, we decided to meet with Father Steve at the Silver Mirror restaurant in Struthers, Ohio, for breakfast before we went back to Pennsylvania. Everybody was on time, and we were seated quickly since the restaurant was not busy after the holiday. As we sat down, Father Steve noticed an older gentleman sitting alone looking like he had lost his best friend. My brother always seemed to notice people in distress, perhaps this was from his training as a priest, but he quickly brought this to our attention. He went on to say, "Maybe he is just down on his luck, maybe he has no family, maybe he didn't even have a meal for Thanksgiving, or maybe he just doesn't have enough money to buy breakfast, since he only had a cup of coffee." My wife thought Father Steve was joking, just trying to get me to react to this situation, and I dismissed him and ordered my breakfast. Father Steve would not give up. He kept looking over at this man and he was making me feel guilty that I was enjoying my breakfast without consideration for this person who was sitting alone. As we were nearing the end of our meal, my brother strongly suggested that I should do a random act of kindness and buy this stranger a meal, with no questions asked. His persistence paid off and I asked the waitress to provide this man with the best breakfast they had and to give the check to me. As we were leaving the restaurant, I went over and told the stranger, "Happy Thanksgiving, breakfast is on me." He was surprised and I had to look away when I saw tears well up in his eyes. Father Steve was smiling, and he was satisfied that this issue was resolved. When I think back on this incident, I realized it was just another one of Father Steve's life lessons about paying forward, doing unto others as you would have them do unto you, and being thankful for what you have.

Father Steve's sister, Margie.

MARGIE

Her children rise up and call her blessed;
her husband, too, praises her:
—Proverbs 31:28 (NABRE)

Life began on June 6, 1953, for me and I've been blessed since that very day. My wonderful life started with a wonderful childhood which led to a beautiful adulthood. God blessed me with a wonderful husband who I will be married to for forty-five years on June 17, 2023, and three amazing sons, Michael (Mikey), Anthony (Tony), and Joseph (Joey). My sons are very close to me, and each one is different. If I was to spend some separate quality time with them, we would do some different things. If I spent time with Mikey, an attorney, we would definitely bake something. We are very proud of our successful apricot *kolach*. We'd talk about gardening and our love for flowers since he is a master gardener. We enjoyed working on this book together, and it was exciting when he told me, "You might have something here, Mom. Send it in." If I spent time with Tony, a captain in a police department, we would probably go fishing out on the Mount Pleasant Pier, compare our gardens, and enjoy country music somewhere. Tony and I would most likely take a ride to downtown Charleston, get a bite to eat, and shop at the outdoor marketplace. We wouldn't leave without buying a famous praline. If my time was spent with Joey, who is a chef, I would be watching him cook, trying to learn some new cooking techniques. We'd definitely go fishing in his backyard and check out his gardens. Joey would never let me leave Savannah without a fancy caramel apple. Christmas would come up in any discussion that we have because we both live for this holiday.

God continued to bless me even more. I began my love of taking care of children by working at a day care and learning center. God respected my love for children and helped me to land a job at Saint Anne School where I was the director and prekindergarten teacher. It was the best job ever! I started the job with a handful of children, maybe five, and by the third year I was able to add another class because the enrollment now consisted of fifty prekindergarten children. The job brought me total enjoyment and I loved going to work. How many people really love their job? After five years, I was offered a job at Summit Academy, an alternative learning school for children who were diagnosed with ADHD, autism and behavioral issues. I had to think a lot about my decision to leave my favorite school, but the enrollment in the upper grades was dwindling and I wasn't sure where the future of the school was headed. So I accepted the job and to my delight found another school of my dreams. My job was to teach social skills to these children and work with their behaviors. In six years, I may have learned more from these children than they even learned from me. I loved watching them learn and become more responsible for their lives, by making better behavioral decisions. I loved both of those jobs and thought my life was complete.

I soon realized that it wasn't complete until I was blessed with three daughters-in-law, Risa, Stefanie, and Rachel, who all get along so beautifully with each other and me. They respect me, spoil me, have fun with me, and we all love each other. How many people can say that about their daughter's-in-law? If I spent the day with Risa, we would probably go to a fine-dining restaurant and maybe enjoy a mimosa. There would definitely be some shopping at a little boutique where she would treat me. An elegant and exciting spa visit would definitely be included in our day. She's fancy like that. She has also included me in her adventurous travel plans throughout the years. If I spent the day with Rachel, we would probably go to a fun spa for a pedicure and some pampering, and maybe we'd buy some new makeup. We'd enjoy lunch at a cute little outdoor restaurant. We'd spend quality time discussing life, our families, and how we can make the best of living our lives spiritually and happily. She likes little quotes, like I do, to get her through the day. A day with Stefanie would consist of lots of chatting between the two of us. We may be discussing the Bible, new healthy ideas, exercising, or simply our families. A spa visit would also be enjoyed. If she was at my house, we would sit by the firepit in the winter, maybe listening to some country music, and enjoy a warm beverage because she enjoys the cold weather and snow, like I do. My three sons text daily keeping in touch with each other about what their wives would call trivial nonsense. If one of them is dealt with an issue that they need to manage, the other two are all out of sync. Another huge blessing is that my sons and their wives all get along and take good care of each other!

God still had five more blessings for me. He chose to send me five beautiful grandchildren, Vincent (Vinny), Isabella (Bella), Caleb, Gianna (Gigi), and Alaina (Ali), who helped my husband and I get through the last ten years. There's a love that you have for your spouse and your child, but there is a different kind of love that a grandparent has for their grandchild. It is simply pure, precious, and priceless. The initials of my granddaughters are tattooed on my ankle with flowers. My husband has the initials of our grandsons tattooed on his upper arm. No matter where we go, we feel as though our grandchildren are right there with us. Whether it is a trip to the grocery store, traveling, attending Mass, or simply going to get some ice cream, we have our five favorite little people with us. My sixth favorite person is a teenager, my nephew, Jacob. He's a star when it comes to sports but stays humble, even when his play makes the winning point. He excels at baseball, basketball, soccer, and football. He loves when we can come to any of his games to watch him play. He's respectful, happy, and a lot of fun to be with. He's the best nephew anyone can ask for. He is actually more like a grandson to us than a nephew. Since Jacob is a teenager, we can envision our grandchildren growing up and now have an idea of what we can look forward to. My five grandchildren love him and always ask when they will get to see Jacob again. My sons and daughter's-in-law all take care of each other's children too. I get to share my faith, my love of Jesus, and my "love of Christmas" gene with them. At Thanksgiving last year, my five grandchildren and I made Christmas/ Happy Birthday cards for Jesus, drawing pictures by using markers, crayons and lots and lots of glitter. The children worked very hard using their creativity and all the imagination that they had. My oldest grandson even drew Jesus on the cross. I guess he wanted Jesus to know what was ahead of him. It was awesome for me to send a Christmas card to Jesus too. I mailed them off to Bethlehem at the local post office where the postal worker spent twenty minutes trying to find the proper address. The six people waiting behind me were very patient with me when they heard the conversation that the postal worker was having with me, I guess they all love Jesus too. The customs card had my address on it and the Christmas cards have never been returned to me, so my grandchildren and I believe that Jesus did receive them. How blessed am I to get to do an activity like that with all five of them at one time? I was also able to share a new Christmas tradition with my grandchildren. I just recently learned about the Peace Light of Bethlehem. In Austria a

child flies to Bethlehem to light a lantern from a flame burning at the star of the Church of the Nativity, in Bethlehem. This star is in the cave that marks the spot where Jesus was born. The child then flies with the explosion-proof lantern. It then travels to more than twenty countries in Europe as well as the Americas. It is part of a charitable mission for handicapped children and people in need. This lighted candle made its way to my neighborhood Christian store where I was able to light my candle from the Bethlehem candle to bring to my home. I was then able to take a candle that was pre-lit from my home and relight it in the houses of my grandchildren. Thus, on Christmas Eve, we all lit our candles knowing that our candles that were lit were from the birthplace of Jesus. What a beautiful Christmas! They're all the love of my life and they continually brighten my day. It could be a simple text message about them, a picture, a card, a phone call, or an unexpected package. If we can't see them, it is great to FaceTime with them because their happy little faces can even make the worst day seem all better. They send samples of their artwork to decorate Father Steve's room. It's simple and colorful artwork, but enough to brighten his day. My husband and I get to travel with our sons, their wives and our grandchildren when Father Steve is doing well. We've been to the Carolinas, Georgia, Tennessee, New York City, New Hampshire, Maine, and even to Italy.

 Vinny, my oldest grandson, is eleven years old and lives in South Carolina. I was there the day he arrived home from the hospital. I would have Vinny in my arms as my son walked in the door from work. He would simply ask me, "You didn't hold him all day, did you?"

 My quick response was "No."

 Of course, I did hold him all day long. Isn't that what grandchildren are for? Technically, I did put him down to make a cup of tea. He is now almost as tall as I am, so I can't really carry him around anymore.

 We do have a nightly ritual when I visit. We may start with a story, and then we say our prayers, always starting with Father Steve. Next comes the entire family and his dog, Scarlet. The relaxing part comes next, which is his favorite back rub while listening to "Christmas Canon" and "Hallelujah," which is our special time together. He also enjoys a shopping spree at Walmart with me. Vinny loves a Dunkin' Donuts visit with me and a fun time at his dock where we wait patiently, trying to catch a fish. He is originally from New Jersey, so he is slowly becoming a Southerner. He is recently very proud to share the news with me that he was just voted as the student council representative for his fifth-grade class. He loves collecting "stuff" just like I do.

Bella, who is my oldest granddaughter, is nine years old and lives in South Carolina. She loves her gymnastics class, and look out when she's about to do a cartwheel. There's no stopping her. She loves a trip to the Isle of Palms to swim and play in the sand. She has just asked me to teach her how to sew on my sewing machine because she wants to make a blanket. I already know how I'll spend my next visit with her when she comes to Ohio. We will be visiting the store and picking out the perfect fabric to use for her very first sewing lesson. Ironically, my first project was a blanket too. It was a blanket for my firstborn child, Mikey. I'm not sure if her feet will even touch the ground to reach the foot pedals, but it will be fun and endearing watching her sew her first stitches on the Singer sewing machine that my husband bought for me forty-four years ago. My mother will be smiling from heaven, hoping the "sewing gene" will be passed on to her. Bella loves jewelry and keeps a little box in her backpack with spare jewelry in case she forgets to put some on in the morning. That's my kind of a girl. She also loves a good Hallmark Christmas movie. We both love Christmas, and last year, Bella and her family sent me a new Christmas Advent wreath for Mike and me to celebrate the season. My five grandchildren look forward to their Christmas calendars that I send them every year.

Caleb, who is six years old. is Bella's brother. He's a neat little guy with his own idiosyncrasies and special rules. He's very disciplined, only eating things on certain days and doing things only in certain ways. He will even iron his own clothes if his doesn't like the outfit that someone picked out for him. He's likes his clothes nice and warm, straight from the ironing board. It might be crazy to have ironing in common with a six-year-old, but I love to iron too and find it very relaxing. Caleb is an extremely creative first-grader. When he does artwork, which he loves, he has details on the whole page. There is no white space in his artwork. Since I love artwork, I willingly join in with him for an art activity. Caleb is a wonderful ice hockey player in the South Carolina Little Rays hockey team. He recently joined a baseball team and loves sliding into first base just to get dirty. Being a very disciplined little boy, he is doing very well at sports—indoors and outdoors. Caleb loves when we join him in a trip to the waterpark. Caleb and his sister have an enormous collection of stuffed animals, spending time each night deciding which one to sleep with. He says that I make famous Christmas cookies and wants to know where I hide the recipe in case something happens to me. He wants it to be our secret.

Gianna (who is six years old) and her sister, Ali (who is four years old), are my granddaughters who live in Georgia. They are different but love some of the same things. They are my special little Christmas elves who love Christmas as much as I do. Little Ali was seen sporting Christmas-tree earrings in August, something I would probably do. Gianna collects Nativity sets and probably has more than I do. They love a good Christmas movie and enjoy the Nativity scene at the cathedral in downtown Savannah. They both love when I read books to them, especially when we act them out. It's always a toss-up as to which is their favorite: *The Three Little Pigs*, *The Three Little Kittens*, or *Little Red Riding Hood*. If you say that you are going to a spa, they are in the car before you, anxiously waiting to get a pedicure and deciding on the color of polish.

After a pedicure one day, I introduced the girls to fine dining. They loved eating at a table covered with a tablecloth and using their best manners. They understood how you need to act differently from when you eat at the local Dairy Queen. They really enjoyed themselves. They are very much like me and love their jewelry and all the things that girls love. The three of us love to bake cookies or muffins and maybe make a pizza. All three of us love to fish in their backyard and maybe later go to Leopold's to get some ice cream when we are done. We can go to their housing development's pool to cool off from the hot Georgia heat. We love to visit the Savannah River

Walk to watch the fancy boats go by. We take a break from the heat to dance and play in the sprinklers. A trip to the Tybee Island beach is the best time too. Whether we are building castles in the sand or playing in the ocean waves, we are definitely having fun. Gianna loves to entertain the sun bathers at the beach with her cartwheels in the sand. She begins with a very serious gymnast pose that she learned in her gymnastics class that she takes in the evening. Ali, on the other hand, would rather impress the onlookers with her ballerina poses that she learned in preschool ballet class. A walk along the beach is always expected just to see what treasures we can come up with. We won't leave the beach without something to eat, ice cream, and definitely a souvenir. The two sleepy girls will snooze the whole way home. What a beautiful way to spend a day in the South.

My world is centered around a three-word mantra all beginning with the letter *H*. My three special words are *holy*, *healthy*, and *happy*. I believe using these three words is the best way to live my life every day. This way, I'm taking care of my soul, body, and mind every day by following a lifestyle like this. To learn to live a holy life, one needs to develop the characteristics of humility, love, tolerance, discipline, peace, and faithfulness. I try to work on improving these six characteristics in my life each day and yes, it is a lot of work. A holy day can be spent by saying a simple prayer for maybe even a stranger that I see struggling in some way. It could consist of a quick prayer as I watch an ambulance flying down the road with a helpless person inside of it. The ambulance driver needs some prayers too for a safe trip. Holy days can consist of morning Mass or maybe a monetary donation to a good cause. Worrying about other people over yourself is pleasing to God.

The second letter *H* word of my daily mantra, *healthy*, is sometimes a struggle. It involves what to eat and what not to eat. It's almost just like choosing between right and wrong. Eating salad over a juicy cheeseburger or hot dog that just came off the grill is a choice nobody wants to make. To complete this healthy mantra exercise comes into play. Some days exercise comes easy and other days that could be a struggle too. Morning walks in the park are the best! I can exercise and say a few prayers covering two letter *H* words in an hour. When it's hot and I'm tired, I still try to manage to pull it off daily.

Of course, *happy* is the simplest of all letter *H* words. I'm a simple person, so it doesn't take a whole lot to make me happy. Many of my happy moments are spent with my husband. I have a bedroom dedicated to my five grandchildren and each wall is dedicated to each little family. Each wall is painted a different color. The wall is covered in their pictures, artwork, railroad tracks, trains, ballerinas, hockey pictures, ice skating pictures, princess wall stickers, and fishing pictures. Colorful shelves, fancy picture frames and bulletin boards adorn the walls. Books, dolls, and all their favorite things are added to their space regularly. Each wall stands for everything that each of my grandchildren loves. Pictures are updated once a year. Now this is one happy place to be, and I could just sit on the floor, look around at all the walls, and I know that my five grandchildren are with me right then and there. Once again, I'm so very blessed!

Margie's family.

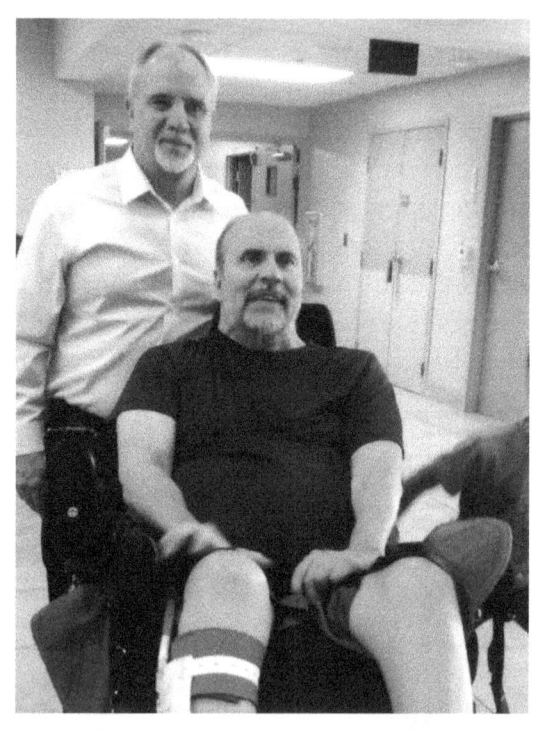

Father Steve and his brother, John.

JOHN

Hear, my son, and receive my words, and the years of your life shall be many. On the way of wisdom I direct you, I lead you on straight paths. When you walk, your step will not be impeded, and should you run, you will not stumble. Hold fast to instruction, never let it go; keep it, for it is your life.
—Proverbs 4:10–13 (NABRE)

When Margie phoned me and said she's writing a book about our brother, Father Steve, I immediately felt there was definitely a story to be shared. Many thoughts flooded my mind, from our time growing up together, my visits home and his visits to California. A previous phone call on November 13, 2013, was not as spirited. It was a tragedy. I cannot even recall who phoned me, but I only can remember the fear of flying back to Ohio not knowing what to expect. Although I had settled down in Southern California in 1986, each visit home always left me with the feeling we had never been apart. But of late, the visits have all revolved around something unpleasant. My father and mother's passing and the immediate need to see my brother, to be by his side and offer whatever I could. I left that visit with so many unanswered questions which continued for so many years and I'm sure still are on his mind.

My time with my family in Ohio has been limited. From 1979–1985 I was in the USMC, then in 1986, I moved to Southern California to work in the aerospace industry where I presently reside. My time with Father Steve has been limited. My trips to Ohio prior to the accident always included spending a day with him at his parish which included some great conversations. I was amazed how everyone he encountered greeted us with smiles and nothing but joy and inclusion. He truly is loved by all he has served, and that number continues to grow.

Today, his accident seems so far in the past that the miles that separate us create a feeling of regret. Regret that I did not do more, regret that my visits were short and that I truly miss him both as he is and how he was—such a joy to be around, full of love, peace and always a guiding force. I must admit, although the Bible says the Lord works in mysterious ways, how unfair that a representation of himself must endure a massive hardship after only helping others for his entire life. Father Steve's acceptance of his cross always helps me to continue to get up when I feel I am faced with uncertainty. I try to understand that he is helping others get through similar issues with hope, but I feel he would have had an even greater impact had this not occurred. Maybe the point is that although I have wondered if he could have helped more people if he was never in the accident, I now see that he has been able to provide help and inspiration to those in extremely difficult situations by fighting through his own adversity. Otherwise, I have not been able to wrap my head around this.

Recently, I experienced a serious health issue, and I was scared. My thoughts lead me back to the sufferings my brother faced. How he fought through extremely difficult health issues repeatedly and yet continued to strive forward teaching us that the Lord never turns his eyes from us. His place in my heart continues each day as I listen to a daily TV Mass every morning. There are readings about Saint Stephen, and it makes me smile as I feel they are reading about my brother. I cannot explain what occurs during the time I sit alone listening, but I do feel a sense of comfort facing the day. Father Steve has continued to impact my life through his perseverance and example both in my conscious and subconscious thoughts.

Growing up, being six and eight years younger than my brothers, they always found a way to include me in their sporting activities. Father Steve and Charlie would get on their knees and we would play football together in our living room. I, of course, was allowed to stand and I would do my best to run through them to score a touchdown. We played at "oak" stadium, which was just a grass lot next to a neighbor's family house. I was able to wear my full football gear with helmet included and they did their best to make me feel the real football pain. God, I really do miss those days. We would go down in the basement, put multiple pairs of our winter socks on our hands, and we would box. Me standing upright and Steve on his knees. Sometimes one of us paid the price, but ultimately mom would reprimand them for beating me up! So, you go through life with your siblings sharing all kinds of things. Father Steve helped me get my first job cleaning St. Matthias church. He was a great example of discipline and always took good care of me.

You know, some days it can be quite a burden to think of what Father Steve has been through and what little I feel I have done for him and my family dealing with this tragedy. My sister Margie and her husband, Mike, have continually been by his side, whether he was friendly that day or not. They are a blessing for him and for the rest of the siblings as they continue to be of service through the good days and the bad days. I always pray for him that the good Lord would take good care of him, although I feel he was not dealt the hand he deserved.

John and his wife, Andrea.

Father Steve and his sister, Elizabeth.

ELIZABETH

"Many are the woman of proven worth,
but you have excelled them all."
—Proverbs 31:29 (NABRE)

Where to Start

I was asked by my amazing sister, Margie, to write a chapter about our brother, Father Steve. It seemed simple, since we have so many stories and we are such a close family. However, I ruminated about it for some time, trying to make my chapter not a memoir, but then what? Am I to write about him, my relationship with him and how his accident impacted us, him or the family? I struggled a lot with how to frame my chapter, leaving me sitting in my office one late night, deciding that I should just write. And here I am.

The story begins with me and my siblings, who are fairly older than me, about around sixteen plus years older. I was a bit of a surprise, and my siblings were almost out of the house, out to college and exploring the years of adulthood. My fondest memories are having my siblings back "home" on Sundays and holidays. In particular, Steve, a.k.a. Father Steve, would come over every Sunday for football and Sunday dinner. How I couldn't wait for that! To have him over and go outside with me to throw around a ball was the best. We were a super competitive family and were never bored. The laughter filled the house beyond belief-a memory I will never forget.

I obviously grew up and moved along with my life, always close in proximity to my brother. We talked, but I always wished we talked more. As I evolved and had a son, Jacob, Father Steve and I grew closer. We lost our parents and that resonated with us very much.

Now I could go on for a long time about stories, but again, this is not a memoir. What is important is that awful day when I received a phone call from my sister about an accident. It sounds like a movie, felt like a movie, but sadly, was not a movie. I was informed that our brother had a bad accident and was "paralyzed." Not sure what that meant, I left work and drove an hour, not sure what to expect. From that point, things changed. Now *changed* is a strong word. But that's what happened. I often look back at that day and that year and struggle with the why. The next many years were a whirlwind of hospitals, and so many emotions to fill a warehouse. Driving to the hospital with coffee and a donut before work, hoping for a good visit, was the goal of the day. I am amazed that after all these years, guess what? Father Steve is here, alive and with us. Again, not a memoir.

My son Jacob will be thirteen years old soon. He grew up experiencing the ups and downs of this accident. I asked Jacob to describe Father Steve. His adjectives were: funny, silly, loving and special. The last one meant the most. Jacob said his best memories were when Father Steve rode his motorcycle up to our house and hid in the Ivy in the backyard, playing hide and seek. Jacob was only three to four years old and remembers this like it was yesterday. Another favorite was Jacob's First Holy Communion. I did not remind him of the time that he was sitting on Father Steve stomach in the hospital when he pulled out his feeding tube!!!! (ouch). When I've been having a quiet discussion about Father Steve with my sister or others, Jacob is fully aware, gets sad, and asks, with a cracking voice, "Is he okay?" Father Steve means the world to this boy. He has taught him humility, patience and empathy, as well as resilience.

If you know my family, you know that everyone would want to be a part of it. I'm beyond grateful for every member of my family and would never be where I am without them. They carry me through good and bad days and Steve is always the constant.

Because this is not a memoir, I want to call out to a few people. My sister and brother-in-law, Margie and Mike—I could never have cared as much for our dear brother as you. I tried hard to do the best I could, an hour away, and know you carried the ball every day. For that, I am more than grateful. And to you, Father Steve, Jacob and I have a few things to say:

> Don't stop believing and praying.
> Stay with us to experience everything life has to
> offer, even if it is tricky now and then.
> We love you, and we are so grateful you continue to be in our lives.
> You taught us to appreciate every little piece
> of life, and we will do that forever.
> You made us realize how lucky we are and
> how we cannot ever disrespect life.
> And most importantly, love and embrace life.

As I write this, I realized that my words are coming quickly. I think this is what journaling is all about. But what this chapter is about is for my brother Father Steve. Who else would be paralyzed from the chest down, lying in bed with a SUPER HOT iron inches from his face and chest and erratically ironing fall leaves on wax paper to hang somewhere in his room.

This is my brother. The best, ever!
We love you, Steve,
Always and forever. xoxoxo Elizabeth and Jacob

Elizabeth and her son, Jacob.

Father Steve and his uncle, Father George.

FATHER GEORGE

As you have anointed their father, anoint them also as my priests. Thus, by being anointed, shall they receive a perpetual priesthood throughout all future generations.
—Exodus 40:15 (NABRE)

Father George was my dad's brother who was a Catholic priest in the Diocese of Youngstown. My dad and his whole family were extremely proud of Father George and truly respected the work that he did for God, his family, and the community.

He probably only stood about five feet tall but was as powerful as a steam roller. It was hard to believe that such a loud voice could come out of such a small guy. He was loved by all because of his good heart and generosity. He was a very religious priest, and everyone respected him. I remember him smiling all the time. Parishioners and the whole community loved him.

He was a staple in our lives, and he was all about family. We all loved him dearly. Awesome would be the word to describe him and he was also a beautiful role model for my family, but especially to my brother. He baptized some of the family members, married us, and buried a few family members too.

We always wanted to visit him and couldn't wait for him to come to our house. He came over very often and he was a super generous priest. After his church picnics were over, he would come to our house with popsicles, candy, prizes, and whatever else was left over from the picnic that he had at his parish. It was like having Santa Claus coming to your house in the summer, except he didn't wear a red suit—he wore all black with a white collar. He also made Christmas the best time ever. You put your order in before Christmas and whatever you wanted, you received. It was like Santa Claus coming again because that's exactly what you got.

He was a pastor at many parishes, and they were all close by, so we were able to go and join him in the celebration of Mass fairly often. His homilies were down to earth, and he touched everyone's heart as he preached at the pulpit. You could barely see him, but you could sure hear him. He mesmerized people as they listened to him.

It is said that he especially enjoyed his last assignment as chaplain of Saint Joseph's healthcare center in Warren, Ohio. He was affectionately known as Father Sunshine and by some as the "candy man." He would push a cart around full of candy and pass it out to everyone, family, patients, and staff. He said that this job was his most satisfying of his almost fifty-year career because the hospital is an environment where priests are needed. He said that he believed that there was no more needy of a place for a priest than to be in a hospital. There are sick people in need of physical and spiritual healing. The family members were there in need of hope and the doctors, nurses, and staff were there in need of prayer. I'm sure he would be so very proud of my brother right now who is in a healthcare environment. At this healthcare environment Father Steve can take care on the spiritual needs of the patients and their families like he did.

When Father George passed away, all our relatives were able to meet and join in prayer. We were all encouraged to pick out some of Father George's treasures that he embraced for so long to be taken home with us to remember him by. I picked out his Bible and I picked out *The Pieta*, by Michelangelo. This is the statute which features Mary holding Jesus's deceased body. It's a beautiful statue made from marble and sits on my fireplace hearth. Every day, at some point, I remember Father George.

Father Steve spreading Christmas cheer in Ohio.

HEAVEN'S ANGELS

> The Lord bless you and keep you! The Lord let his
> face shine upon you, and be gracious to you! The
> Lord look upon you kindly and give you peace!
> —Numbers 6:24–26 (NABRE)

Father Steve and two other friends of his, who were also priests, rode motorcycles together and belonged to what people called Heaven's Angels. Father rode a 2011 Suzuki Boulevard. He had been riding for thirty-one years, a great hobby for him. He tells us that a hobby takes time, talent, and treasure.

As for the cost of the motorcycles, the priests said that they save up just like lay people do. When they ride, they feel close to God and nature. Praying goes along with riding the bikes because riding in the open air gives them a good time to reflect.

The priests have experienced and conducted motorcycle blessings. The priests say that you can feel the fellowship and how it brings people closer together as a community. The priests use the book of blessings and take passages from it to bless the motorcycle riders and their bikes. The motorcycles are blessed whether they're traveling for business or pleasure.

These blessings provide a chance for the priests to encourage safety. Father Steve says that he always likes to wear bright colors so that he's noticed on the road. Speaking of bright colors, Father Steve was once spotted on Mahoning Avenue in Youngstown, Ohio, wearing a Santa suit and riding his bike. Christmas was just around the corner, and he wanted to spread some Christmas cheer. Little children stared out their windows and were amazed when Santa was driving past them on a motorcycle. He would do whatever he could do to put smiles on people's faces, especially children. And you guessed it, he nailed it this time. He was a little kid at heart and seeing children waving from their car windows made him smile too.

We got a phone call from him and knew that he was out and about on his bike, so we became concerned immediately. He lost his Santa hat while riding and he called out to us to ask if we could go and try to search for it. Of course, we said yes, and the mission began. We looked up and down Mahoning Avenue. We retrieved his Santa hat. In the meantime, he was sitting behind a restaurant because he didn't want anyone to see Santa without his hat. He took the hat, jumped back on his bike, and took off almost like Santa on his sleigh. He was back on his mission, spreading Christmas cheer to everyone. That's what he was all about!

PRISON MINISTRY

For I was hungry and you gave me food, I was thirsty and you gave me drink, a stranger and you welcomed me, naked and you clothed me, ill and you cared for me, in prison and you visited me. Then the righteous will answer him and say, "Lord when did we see you hungry and feed you, or thirsty and give you drink? When did we see you a stranger and welcome you, or naked and clothed you? When did we see you ill or in prison, and visit you?" And the king will say to them in reply, "Amen I say to you, whatever you did for one of these least brothers of mine, you did for me."
—Matthew 25:35–40 (NABRE)

Father Steve replaced Father Nick Shori at St. Paul's Parish. Before Father Shori left, he got Father Steve interested in the prison ministry. This ministry was right up Father Steve's alley because a prison ministry would be a challenge and he loved a good challenge. The prison was a maximum-security prison in Youngstown, Ohio.

Prior to Father Steve's visits to the prison, he would carefully pack up his prison ministry bag with all the sacred essentials that he would need and placed it in the trunk of his Grand Am. The bag contained everything that he would need to celebrate Mass with the prisoners.

My brother celebrated Mass with maybe four to six prisoners at one time. At times he would just sit and talk with the prisoners. Some of the prisoners were baptized and confirmed by him. He was there to spread his faith and to share all that he knew about Jesus, and he was great at that. He was there during the holidays to sing Christmas carols with them. The prisoners he ministered to did not view him as the stereotypical priest since he was a weightlifter. This probably helped the prisoners to resonate with him a little easier. About fifty out of the five hundred prisoners there were Catholic. The Catholic denomination was the one mostly represented at the prison with other priests and lay people visiting during the week.

The prisoners were at all different levels depending on the crime that they were incarcerated for. Some of the lower-level security prisoners were able to sit at a table, shackled of course. Some were in booths that were locked, and the Holy Eucharist was administered by way of a little portal.

When the prisoners are released from this prison, they are given some cash, a shirt, pants, a bus ticket to wherever they were going, and any belongings that they came with, if any. This was an important ministry that Father Steve truly enjoyed. He worked his hardest trying to reach out to these prisoners to give them some encouragement, hope, and determination. He knew that what they were about to encounter when they left there would not be easy. Getting back into society would be tough, especially the way society judges people.

This is the prison where Father Steve was driving to on the day of his accident. When he didn't make it there, the prisoners all found out about what happened to him. The prisoners made beautiful cards and sent them to him. The prisoners wrote beautiful letters from their hearts and designed truly incredibly beautiful covers on their cards. His first visit back with them was a very touching and empowering visit for Father Steve and the prisoners.

Father Steve would take my husband on a few of his prison visits. When Mike did not go, the nurses accompanied him. They had to be trained before they were permitted to go into the prison with him. Father Steve carried a special chip that got him into the prison. This ministry was not only important but rewarding for my brother.

After my brother's accident, Bishop George Murry, the past bishop of the Diocese of Youngstown said, "God loves everyone, even those who are imprisoned. Let us not miss an opportunity to place our hands in his by doing his work. We do prison ministry out of respect for the will of the Lord and to carry on the mission of Father Steve."

THANKSGIVING

> Therefore, my brothers, when you come
> together to eat, wait for one another.
> —1 Corinthians 11:33 (NABRE)

Thanksgiving has always been one of my brother's favorite holidays, especially since the word *Eucharist* means "thanksgiving." It's also central to his Catholic faith.

Father lived at a Rehabilitation Center in Kent, Ohio, for a short period where he met up with an inspirational gospel singing group. They came to the activity room for some entertainment for the patients. The song "So Much to Thank Him For" was written by Kevin Spencer and sung by the gospel group. There were about four in the band and one singer was in a wheelchair. The song brought my brother to tears as he realized all that he had to be thankful for. He met the band and asked them for their prayers and a blessing. It kind of made their day when they found out that he was a priest and that he wanted their blessing.

He said that despite his current health issues his thankful list was long. Looking back on his family background, the love, the concern, the enjoyment, the good times, the celebrations and the closeness of our family was his priority. He was raised in a great environment on the south side of Youngstown, blessed with a great education at St. Matthias School, Cardinal Mooney High School, and Youngstown State University. He believes that this has all formed him to be what he is today. He thought back at all the great times he had and the trips he had made to Italy and the Holy Land. He won't forget his motorcycle trips out West and down South.

On Thanksgiving, my brother would reminisce about all the delicious meals he had eaten in his whole life, remembering the time after surgery when food or drinking was prohibited.

He is grateful for Mount St. Mary's Seminary and the education that he received which resulted in him being ordained a priest. He says that he's been blessed and graced by God as a priest since he celebrates the Eucharist and is an integral part of the fabric of many of his parishioners' lives. People have called him when they were going through a divorce, when they were getting married, when they needed him to visit someone, when a friend or family member needed anointing of the sick, planning a funeral, and participating in graduations and First Holy Communions. Father says, "How blessed I am!" He said that he took it for granted that he was the fabric of people's lives for some very, very important occasions. People entrusted their lives and their faith to him.

After receiving cards and letters since the accident, he has realized even more that being part of their lives and letting him into their lives is more than just talking about football or the weather. It is talking about faith and its challenges.

When he thinks back to the song, "So Much to Thank Him For," he now tries to focus each day on a certain part of what he is thankful for. It brings him back to that tune in the midst of his struggles, difficulties, and illnesses. He tries to keep himself balanced and shows his appreciation to the good Lord for what he has given him. This has been an important part of his healing!

THE CHOSEN

Then Jesus said to his disciples, "Whoever wishes to come after
me must deny himself, take up his cross, and follow me.
—Matthew 16:24 (NABRE)

Dallas Jenkins has presented to the world *The Chosen*, the movie following Jesus as he gathers his disciples, heals the needy, and sacrifices himself for the sake of humanity. It's a movie that can be life changing for most and the effects from this movie are unquantifiable.

On a Saturday, I got a phone call from my brother asking if Mike and I wanted to join him at the movie theater to see *The Chosen*. This is a very powerful movie that touched my heart and soul. My brother, his nurse, Mike, and I thoroughly enjoyed the movie.

The movie we watched was season 3 of *The Chosen*. Episode 2, in my mind and heart was very touching and I feel that this is my favorite episode. In this episode, Jesus commissioned his twelve disciples and prepares them to be sent out in pairs of two to preach, heal, and to teach God's word. One of the chosen apostles who is called Little James has a problem with his leg and uses a cane. James questions Jesus about why he has not been healed yet especially after he has seen Jesus heal so many other people. He wonders how he can go out and preach about the God who has not even healed him yet. It was very hard for him to comprehend this and he questioned Jesus about this.

Jesus explains to James that yes it would be a good story for him to go out and heal people and preach about Jesus after he has been healed. But Jesus reminded James, to think of the story that he would have when he goes out into the world with a handicap and still will preach God's word even though he has not been healed. Jesus tells

James, "Oh, what a sight. I can't wait to hear your stories." Jesus tells little James, "You will be healed. It's only a matter of time." Jesus also reminds James that he will be rewarded in heaven. The scene reminds me so very much of what my brother is going through. Father Steve told me when I wrote this book that I would promise him to never make him out as being a saint. I kept my promise, however, he never mentioned to me that I could not compare him to a disciple. In my heart I see such a correlation here that I need to share. Yes, James has a bad leg, and my brother has two bad legs. James is going out to preach the word of the Lord despite his disability. My brother has been preaching God's word by mouth and by his example despite his disability for ten years.

It would have been a very good story if God had performed a miracle and helped my brother so that he could walk again. After so many years, people would kind of forget about that story and the impact that it had on them at the time. The impact may have lasted only a few years. The miracle would become old news. Now, almost ten years later, Father still has not been healed, but still pushes forward daily by his example of true faithfulness. He has impacted so many lives in ten years by his example of determination and simply the fact that he won't give up. He has gotten people to come back to church, start praying again, and finding the God that they once worshipped and loved. His life right now is an example of a man who trusts what the Lord his God plans to do with his life. He never questions the Lord.

I'm sure James is in heaven with the Lord our God reaping the rewards that Jesus promised him while he was here on earth. Someday, it will be my brother's turn to make it through those pearly gates greeted by Saint Peter, and our mother and father. I hope Father Steve gets to meet little James, shake his hand and say, "We made it!"

TRAVEL

Lord, you have probed me, you know me: you know when I
sit and stand; you understand my thoughts from afar. You sift
through my travels and my rest; with all my ways you are familiar.
—Psalm 139:1–3 (NABRE)

Prior to his accident, my brother loved to travel. Some of his trips involved his ministry. Others were simply for pleasure. Most times, however, his travel combined ministry and pleasure.

When Father Steve visited the Holy Land, he was able to visit the following places: The Garden of Gethsemane, Bethlehem where Jesus was born, the Sea of Galilee, the River Jordan, Jerusalem where Jesus had his Last Supper, and then onto Calvary. He took this trip with a church group. He not only got to visit those places that were important to him, but he was able to share these experiences with another fellow priest and the parishioners from the church that scheduled the Holy Land excursion.

Father Steve loved visiting Italy, with the Vatican being his favorite place. He loved and respected the Sistine Chapel. This place requires silence, and no pictures or videos are permitted. The ceiling was painted by Michelangelo. One of the most talked about frescoes within the Sistine Chapel is the painting where God is reaching out and touching the finger of Adam to give him the gift of life. My brother felt that this truly is a powerful painting! He also loved visiting the Coliseum, standing there imagining the battles between men and animals and the hand-to-hand combat between gladiators. He thought of all the Roman games that were played and all the Christian martyrs that died.

Laredo, New Mexico, was visited by Father Steve, and he said it was a pretty place to visit. He stayed in Laredo at the La Cinta Hotel. He rented a car, drove around town, got a haircut, did some great shopping and found some people grilling outside who made him great corn on the cob on a stick. He was happy with his haircut, which was surprising because I believe my brother can only speak three words in Spanish so I'm not sure how he explained how he wanted his haircut. He was very impressed with some young boys who wanted to shine his shoes. He was not wearing dress shoes, but Nike sneakers, and they said they could take care of them for him. Father said that they weren't kidding because his shoes never looked that great.

For three summers, my brother lived in the Bronx, New York. He was in New York completing his master's degree in religious education at Fordham University. He was able to stay with the Jesuit priests while working on this degree. He loved wearing his Yankee T-shirts while he was there to support their baseball team.

Las Vegas, Nevada, was always a fun time for Father Steve. On many of his trips visiting this city, his family joined him. A niece, four nephews, mother, sister and brothers-in-law all joined Father Steve with the Vegas festivities from swimming, buffet eating, sight-seeing, and a Hawaiian luau.

California was the scene where Father Steve visited his brother, John, and his family, Andrea, Joshua, and Monica a couple of times. Don't you just love unannounced visitors! They loved the time that they got to spend together! Father Steve enjoyed this time meeting his nephew and niece and spending quality time with them.

Charleston, South Carolina, was the setting for Father Steve to visit his nephew, Tony. Father Steve rode his motorcycle on this vacation because it was summertime, and he knew the warm weather would be inviting. The hi-light of the trip was when they visited the Mepkin Abbey, which is a community of Roman Catholic monks. It is surrounded by several miles of river and beautifully preserved and maintained woodland and farmland. He was a little nervous seeing the "watch out for alligator" signs. It was a beautiful place for my brother to pray. He was happy to visit there because it reminded him of a picture that he has on his wall called *God Alone*. He also loved visiting the monastery in Gethsemane, Kentucky. Both monasteries are run by the Trappist monks.

My brother cannot travel far now due to the twenty-four care he requires. Does he miss these trips? Or are the short trips to see family and friends enough for him? It's hard to see my brother limited to pre-planned short trips when he used to be so spontaneous. But as time goes by, I've started to conclude that my brother just likes to be with people-it doesn't have to be far away.

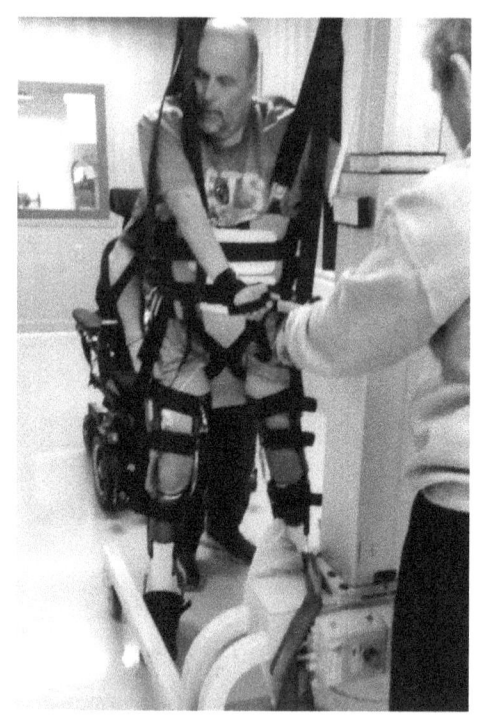

Father Steve as he learns to walk with braces.

WALKING WITH BRACES

Jesus immediately knew in his mind what they were thinking to themselves, so he said, "Why are you thinking such things in your hearts? Which is easier, to say to the paralytic, 'Your sins are forgiven,' or to say, 'Rise pick up your mat and walk? But that you may know that the son of man has authority to forgive sins on earth" he said to the paralytic, "I say to you, rise, pick up

your mat, and go home." He rose, picked up his mat at once, and went away in the sight of everyone. They were all astounded and glorified God, saying, "We have never seen anything like this."
—Mark 2:8–12 (NABRE)

During the course of Father Steve's physical therapy, the physical therapist saw a lot of potential in him and the progress he was making. In part of the process of getting him stronger, Father Steve stood at the parallel bars while the clinician stood in front of him blocking his knees. His nurse was holding him as she stood next to him. After working with him for many weeks, the clinician believed that Father Steve would benefit from a body brace which is used to help people stand and mimic walking by swinging their hips. In order for my brother to start walking with a body brace, a doctor first had to come in and make a plaster cast of him from his waist down to his ankles.

Once the plaster cast was completed, the next step was converting the cast into a brace. The brace was made of metal and leather straps. There were locking and hinging positions at the knees and the brace would fit from the bottom of his feet up to his midchest. Once the brace was completed, we had to get my brother into it. It took a minimum of four people to accomplish this task. To begin with, Father Steve had to lay back in his wheelchair. Four people lifted him, and each one of the four people had to be in position. When someone said "Ready," everyone did what they were supposed to do. It was a little nerve-wracking because no one wanted to be responsible for dropping him or causing my brother any skin damage. Two clinicians and Mike and I would lift him and nervously do our part and slowly rest him in the brace. We would then check his skin and put foam spacers wherever it looked like his skin might rub. Once this was complete, we put a pair of shoes on him, and he was ready to go.

When he was in the brace and back in the wheelchair, we would then have a machine called a LiteGait machine standing in front of him. A LiteGait machine provides postural control and weight bearing assistance for fall-free therapeutic activities. It permits the clinician to be hands-free when working with clients of all functional levels and diagnoses. The design of the LiteGait machine allows body weight support to be directed only when needed, while facilitating normal weight bearing where appropriate. The overhead straps provide postural control and support for symmetric upright positioning even for those who cannot support themselves. It allows patients to safely engage in progressively challenging functional activities early in the rehabilitation process and throughout treatment. It can be used over the ground or over a treadmill.

For Father Steve to stand we had to connect him to two straps that would connect to his brace in four points so that when he stood up, he would be supported so that he would not fall. Once my brother stood, his knees would lock, and we would adjust the height on the LiteGait to determine how much pressure we would put on his feet. We were able to lower the LiteGait to make him do more and more of the work himself. Eventually, he progressed to the point where he would start at one end of the hallway, walk all the way down to the other end, and out the doors into the parking lot. This did not happen overnight, but probably took up to six months. At first, we would measure his progress by how many ceiling tiles he would walk. We eventually started measuring how many floor tiles he would walk as he was getting stronger and more determined to walk the length of the hallway. Once he succeeded in walking the length of the hallway, he continued to walk outdoors in the parking lot. In the parking lot, on one occasion, Father Steve decided he wanted to walk up to the curb on the street. Going to the street was a challenge as it was on an incline and none of us knew if he was strong enough to complete this task. My brother surprised us by making it all the way up the incline to the street. On his next therapy session, he started again, and he went all the way down the hallway, out through the doors, into the parking lot, up the hill to the sidewalk, and then to what we called the upper parking lot. He was a walking machine! He walked in the upper parking lot for approximately another forty to fifty feet where he got tired. After he completed this huge accomplishment, all the staff and therapists, were quite happy with him. As he did this, Father Steve had to move his hips from side to side to mimic walking.

He would need to throw his left hip and then his right hip and his foot would rise just enough so that they would be able to move.

Unfortunately, when the COVID-19 pandemic occurred, therapy ceased, and Father Steve lost all the accomplishments that he had worked so hard for. Again, I wondered, where was my brother? He was progressing towards some form of normalcy and suddenly, it was gone.

You Are a Priest Forever.

WALL OF MEMORIES

May you be blessed by the Lord, maker of heaven and earth.
—Psalm 115:15 (NABRE)

Father Steve's room is a room full of priceless memories.

Gifts from friends and family adorn his walls and shelves. There isn't anything in his room that isn't important to him. Everything is strategically placed on his wall and on his shelves. They all have a special spot. Very important words on the shelf in his room read, "*Tu sei sacerdote in eterno.*" These are Italian words that mean, "You are a priest forever."

A framed collage of Saint Stephen items is placed in the center of one of the walls. The collage includes a holy card with the picture of Saint Stephen on it. Pictures that my brother took while he visited Jerusalem surround the holy card. The story of how and why Saint Stephen was stoned is taken from the Acts of the Apostles and written on this plaque. There's a picture of the building where he was stoned and a picture of the famous gate.

A Christmas Vatican plaque and Last Supper display from Italy rests on his shelf. Two of his favorite religious songs are written out in sheet music, placed on wood, and placed next to the plaques from the Vatican. His two favorite songs are "Amazing Grace" and "The Old Wooden Cross."

Family pictures are displayed on the family wall. Pictures from the day he was ordained to the present are constant memories for him of great memorable times gone by with an unforeseen future ahead of him. At least he had a beautiful past of treasured memories that became the best steppingstones for his future. Now his wheelchair and true faith will get him through whatever the future holds for him.

On one wall, there are two framed pictures that face him as he wakes up and goes to sleep. One of the pictures depicts the song "Let There be Peace on Earth." What a very fitting song to be facing my brother, in the morning and at night. He lives in a very peaceful place with peaceful nurses in a peaceful environment. Next to it on the wall is a matching frame with "The Prayer of Saint Francis." The two pictures focus on peace. "The Prayer of Saint Francis" is a widely known Christian prayer for peace. He has two very powerful peace symbols, a prayer and a song. A beautiful way to start and end every day.

This same wall also looks almost like a wall from a grade school classroom. Father's nephew and great nephews and great nieces paint, color, and draw pictures for Father Steve. They also send in some of their artwork that they do at school. They're excited to do it and he is just as excited to be on the receiving end. Nothing is more important than innocent artwork from four to twelve-year-olds.

In the very middle of that wall, is a framed picture that my brother won at an auction fundraiser. There's a picture of Jesus holding up bread to heaven. This is the wall that my brother faces when he wakes up in the morning and goes to sleep at night. The comfort of Jesus, the peaceful songs, and his little relative's artwork is worth waking up to and going to sleep to. Sleep time involves his iPad playing either religious music or the sound of rain. Yes, rain, that purified white noise to get you and keep you asleep.

There are stars on his ceiling above his bed that light up at night. Some are placed randomly, and some are in the form of a constellation. Of course, there is a star up there which you can feel represents the Star of Bethlehem. The last time the star was seen in the sky was on March 4, 1226, and the next time it will be seen will be in 2080. The star of Bethlehem was used by the Three Kings to visit Jesus. Maybe the star of Bethlehem could put my brother on the path to follow what God wants him to do for the rest of his life. It's always fun to imagine seeing the Star of Bethlehem in the sky, so why not keep it on the ceiling all the time as a remembrance of the birth of Jesus.

The North Star is considered the anchor of the northern sky. It shines over the North Pole and is commonly seen during the Christmas season. It's like a landmark, but in the sky. It helps people follow and determine direction. It symbolizes direction, guidance, stability, and purpose because of its fixed position relative to other stars. It always remains at almost the same spot in relation to all other stars no matter how much they appear to move around. Isn't looking up at the North Star a peaceful way to fall asleep?

My brother says that the stars remind him of the Bible verse about Abraham and Sarah. Their names were Abram and Sarai, but when the Lord called them in a new way, he changed their names. The Lord tells Abraham that he will give him as many descendants as there are stars in the sky. My brother's ceiling looks like the many descendants that God gave Abraham.

A wooden Sower of the Seed statue is placed on his bookshelf. The statue is of a man holding a basket and throwing seeds. God is represented as the man and the seeds are God's message to us. In the parable, we see Jesus as a Sower of the Seed. Various soils are in our hearts. They can be fertile, rocky, or thorny. We need to keep our soils fertile so that we can cooperate with the Holy Spirit and always be ready to hear his word and spread it. The moral of this parable is how a seed starts to grow in the soil. God's word can encourage us in our soils to lead a life of faith, hope, and trust. It is necessary for us to spread God's word and that is why this Sower of the Seed statue is so important to my brother.

A picture of a few boats with waves all around them is framed with the words, spoken by Jesus, "Come and follow me. And I will make you fishers of men." At once, Jesus's followers left their nets and followed him. A net is hanging on the wall to represent the nets that were used for fishing by the disciples. If my brother lived during the time of Jesus, he would so want to go fishing with him.

Simon and Andrew were approached by Jesus as they were fishing one day, and he told them to come and follow him. He would make them "fishers of men," meaning fishing for others to follow the word of the Lord. Apparently, we don't need to be walking around with a fishing pole, we all just need a good hook to get people to join us and follow God and his word.

Father is an adult "fisher of men," and he loves the sport of fishing. He's great at hooking fish in the lake and great at hooking and catching people to follow God's word. There are times when he is fishing for fish and there are other times when he is fishing for souls. It's a win-win situation for my brother and the souls that he brings to God. It is not necessarily a win-win situation for the fish though, because they may end up being supper that night.

His fishing poles stand in the corner of his room and so, yes, Lord, he is ready to go fishing with you! His tackle box is in the van ready to go anytime. He has a tackle box just like our dad did except his is much smaller. His fishing tackle box is equipped for everything he needs to land the "big one."

He also has a tackle box filled for life. His tackle box for life is somewhat different, except for the hooks. Fishing hooks in his fishing tackle box are used to catch fish whereas the hooks in his tackle box for life are used to catch souls. He often can hook onto the souls of people who need to be brought back into the church if they left it or new souls who haven't found Jesus yet. His tackle box for life is filled with old and new items. It is filled with faithfulness, goodness, generosity, honesty, humility, compassion, integrity, gratitude, loyalty and a friendly smile. Occasionally, he gets out to use the poles or lets his nurses or family use them to try their luck at the sport. He's always ready to go.

There's another framed saying on the wall. It is titled, "And He Shall Be Called…Jesus Christ." Between the words *called* and *Jesus Christ*, there are fifty-three names that Jesus is often called besides Jesus Christ. The names range from the *Advocate* to *the Way, the Truth, and the Life*.

Next to the framed saying is a picture of the Abbey of Our Lady of Gethsemane, Kentucky. This place is a Catholic monastery in the United States. In the House of Trappist, monks have lived, worked and prayed there for almost 170 years. Guests have been received there from the first days when it was founded in 1848. Speaking is permitted in only certain areas. There are woods and fields surrounding the Abbey where people can go to reflect and pray. The words *God Alone* are inscribed on the building in big letters. The phrase "God alone" tells monks and visitors that, yes, God alone is enough in your life.

Jesus the Good Shepherd statue on his shelf represents a shepherd who lays down his life for his sheep and the parable of the Good Shepherd tells us that the shepherd will leave ninety-nine others and will search for the one lost sheep. God will rejoice when he finds that one lost sheep even more than the ninety-nine that didn't go astray. When a sinner returns to God, he celebrates the same way. Jesus as a shepherd will give his own life for his sheep. God has sacrificed his own life for us. What have we done for him?

Saint Francis is another important statue that is on the shelf. My brother also has a very large one that sits in the front of his garden. Saint Francis of Assisi is a patron saint of the poor, animals, and ecology. This statue should help all of us to be present to all the beautiful things that God created for us. His feast day is October 4. Many churches host a blessing of animals on his feast day.

A coffee mug sits on a shelf with the words on it, "Commit to the Lord whatever you do, and your plans will succeed." You can see this in everyday life if you follow and listen to his teachings and the plans that were made will follow through for us. A life of no commitments to the Lord will only end in a life of unsuccessful plans.

A large, beautiful face of Jesus made from burlap was given to Father Steve by friends. It rests on the wall, and I believe he is watching my brother and is doing a wonderful job at it. My brother is living proof of this. This burlap piece of art was bought at a special craft show that makes very unique products and, yes, this is one unique and beautiful piece of art.

A very large picture of the Sacred Heart of Jesus adorns one wall. Father Steve was a janitor at St. Mathias Church during his teenage years. He absolutely loves everything about Saint Mathias. He went to grade school there and served there at Sunday Mass. I believe that St. Matthias helped to make a close relationship with Father Steve and God. He spent a lot of time there working, serving, and learning. In the basement, there was a beautiful picture of the Sacred Heart. The church was in the process of being torn down to build a new one. Father Steve acquired this picture and it followed him on his priestly journey. He took it to the seminary with him and to every place after that. It has never been left behind. It even followed him to the healthcare facility where he lives. The Sacred Heart is one of the most reverent symbols in Roman Catholicism. It represents Christ's love for mankind through his sacrifice on the cross. It is usually depicted as a shining flaming heart, pierced by the lance wound, and encircled by the crown of thorns, surmounted by a cross, and bleeding. My brother has had this picture with him for fifty years.

A beautiful wooden statue on Father Steve's shelf represents the washing of the feet. Jesus washed the disciple's feet and showed that no one is above serving their neighbor. This action of washing the feet on Holy Thursday is important to Father Steve. Throughout many years of his priesthood, he has spent the evening on Holy Thursday washing the feet of parishioners. A few years back before the COVID-19 pandemic, Father Steve was able to go back to one of his former parishes, Immaculate Heart of Mary and spend Holy Thursday with his parishioners. Although he was in his wheelchair, he was able to still wash the feet of his fellow parishioners and participate in the ceremony. It was a beautiful ceremony and people were extremely excited to have him back at the parish and celebrating Holy Thursday with them. It made their Holy Week extra special to them and it made Father Steve's Holy Thursday extra special to him.

There are a few angel statues on his shelf and I'm sure they are there like his guardian angels, protecting him. They stand right next to a few statues of Mary. They are very significant since he was the pastor at Immaculate Heart of Mary Parish. They are sitting next to a metal church that he purchased while visiting Laredo, New Mexico.

Father Steve's Chalice and Ciborium sit on his shelf next to the flag that is folded and framed from our father's casket. He fought in World War II. It is very fitting because our parents bought my brother his first chalice when he was ordained, and it is the chalice that he uses to this day.

There are some of his weightlifting trophies as well while others are in storage. There's a picture of Father Steve when he flipped a tire at the weightlifting contest.

There's is also a shelf above the family wall that holds statues of Matthew, Mark, Luke, and John, the disciples. They stand next to beautiful statues of Jesus and Mary which he had acquired from his uncle, Father George.

Father has two incense burners hanging from the shelf. Incense burners are usually used at funeral masses. The priest will incense the coffin, a sign of honor to the body of the deceased and as a sign of belief of the faithful prayers for the deceased rising to God, symbolic of sanctification and purification. The aroma of the incense can calm the environment and your mind. Father has been known to use the burning of incense at a few funerals and in his garden.

Of course, his love of football is present on those shelves in the form of two footballs. One football is from Youngstown State University, and the other football is from Cardinal Mooney High School. The Cardinal Mooney football was signed by the football players from the school, and it was brought to him after the accident at Saint Elizabeth's Hospital.

Father Steve lifting a six-hundred-pound tire and flipping it while competing at the strongman competition.

WEIGHTLIFTING

This is the day the Lord has made; let us rejoice in it and be glad.
—Psalm 118:24 (NABRE)

Father Steve is a mind, heart, and soul kind of guy. He always takes care of all three of these.

He takes care of his mind by many hours of reading the newspaper and good books. He's quite a news junkie and likes to keep up with whatever is going on. He has two master's degrees, but that will never stop him from learning something new every day.

He takes care of his soul through prayer, administering the sacraments, celebrating Mass and everything else that falls under his ministry.

Father Steve takes care of his heart by exercising. While teaching at Saint Thomas Aquinas school my brother was introduced to the world of weightlifting. He loved football and he got to know the football team and watched them as they did their workouts. He was determined to join in with them and learn the different techniques on how to become stronger.

Father Steve spent one of his summers at Immaculate Heart of Mary church in Austintown, Ohio. He tried to get others involved who were as excited about weightlifting as he was. He spoke to the parish council about a bench press competition at their church festival and how it could raise some money for the church.

The church featured a bench press competition and even had a holiday bench press competition in December. They did this every year for five years. Initially, on Saturday mornings during the festival, the lift contest took place. It was quickly decided that all future lift contests would take place on Saturday evening during the festival, since it drew an exceptionally large crowd. Fifty guys attended the bench press competition and they all received shirts, while trophies were presented to the winners. Almost $900 was raised during the festival and everybody was pleased! All the meets were required to be drug free. Father Steve's bench press was an amazing four hundred pounds!

He loved lifting so much that he traveled to Wintersville, Ohio, and Buffalo, New York, with a weightlifter friend for the meets. He was always looking for a good meet and he wanted everyone to love weightlifting like he did. The competitive edge of my brother was shining through.

I believe my brother was a believer in the quote by George Horace Lorimer, "You've got to get up every morning with determination if you want to go to bed with satisfaction."

Father Steve's weightlifting friend hosts a meet twice a year at Immaculate Heart of Mary to offer a meet for all the weightlifting fanatics. It was sponsored by the World National Powerlifting Federation right in front of the rectory. The meets are still attended by the men who have a passion for the sport thirty years later. My brother still attends a few of the meets to cheer on the lifters. He was not only considered to be an awesome weightlifter, but an awesome cheerleader too. He supported all the lifters, encouraged everyone, and pushed them to their limit. After the Saturday meet, Father Steve would celebrate Mass and everyone would say that his homilies were awesome, and it was said that his voice was even louder than usual. He was still super pumped up from the morning meet. He loved great competition and helping people excel at what they could do to reach their goals was right up his alley.

A strongman contest was held for two years and each year ten men participated. There were five different activities that the weightlifters participated in. The first event was called a tire flip where the contestants had to flip the tire eventually earning them points. Father Steve was able to lift a six-hundred-pound tire and flip it, earning him points. The truck pull was the next challenge, and it was quite the challenge. It was a competition to pull a truck which was timed.

The farmer's walk was the next competition where the competitors had to carry two bars weighing forty pounds plus added weights. The judges measured how far the competitors went and how fast they walked. These all are activity earned points and they were all added up to find out who the winner was.

The next competition, the barrel toss, engaged competitors to throw barrels up and over a banner. The more barrels that they threw over the banner, the more points they earned. This activity was also timed.

The last event required the use of dumbbells. Dumbbells were used by the competitors as they hung freely as long as they could. Men loved all the weightlifting activities that Immaculate Heart of Mary sponsored and all were happy that the money went to the church.

I often wonder if my brother misses these competitions and if the brother I had before the accident would still be here competing. To this day, my brother still lifts weights. He may not bench press four hundred pounds like he did at one time, but whatever he is lifting probably feels like four hundred pounds to him! Maybe my brother is still here.

Father Steve lifting weights at Liberty Healthcare Center.

BEANS, BEANS, AND MORE BEANS

> The one who supplies seed to the sower and bread
> for food will supply and multiply your seed and
> increase the harvest of your righteousness.
> —2 Corinthians 9:10 (NABRE)

My brother loves the story *Jack and the Beanstalk,* by Henry Cole. The moral of the story is to make the best of a bad situation and when opportunity knocks, take advantage of it. The story reminds you to watch who you trust.

He loves the story and how the bean sprout grows up to the sky. It almost looks like a ladder reaching up to heaven. It would certainly be quite a temptation to climb that beanstalk ladder and see what was really up there. In the story, Jack sees a castle when he reaches the top of the beanstalk, but what would we see? Would we get a sneak peek at heaven because that too could sure look like a castle to us? Maybe we would even see someone up there that we knew. Would we be tempted to want to go and stay up there? It could be quite a temptation because life is really tough down here on earth.

My brother loves greens beans, so in his garden we planted green beans. The first year we planted the beans in rows right up in front of the garden and they grew beautifully. Then, he decided he wanted pole beans. I think the child in my brother came out and he wanted to be like Jack in the story. We bought pole beans to plant and bought a fancy climbing apparatus. The beans took off and grew very well. In fact, they grew like crazy climbing up and reaching the top of the five-foot apparatus. There were lots and lots of beans on those plants and he was able to pick them right from his wheelchair.

It was a far cry from the bean plants that Jack planted that reached all the way up to heaven. We couldn't have the climbing device any higher because the beans were planted in a wide-open area and if wind came through, they would be blown right down. My brother had to settle for a very short bean pole ladder, nothing that compared to Jack's.

Beans symbolize immortality and magic powers. Once beans are planted, they can represent resurrection and reincarnation since they grow spiritually upward toward heaven. It is said that if you dream about beans, your dream will symbolize nourishment, earthiness, hope, and trust. Maybe Jack was on to something all along. It will be planting season in Northeast Ohio in a few weeks. Guess who will be out in the garden with us directing us where to plant those pole bean seeds?

And his name won't be Jack!

DEATH AND DYING

Jesus told her, "I am the resurrection and the life; whoever believes in me, even if he dies, will live, and everyone who lives and believes in me will never die. Do you believe this?" She said to him, "Yes, Lord. I have come to believe that you are the Messiah, the Son of God, the one who is coming into the world."
—John 11: 25–27 (NABRE)

Father Steve has taken care of many people throughout his ministry. He has performed many baptisms, funerals, and all the sacraments in between. His ministry doesn't stop there. He has counseled many people throughout his forty-four years of priesthood. People and children often need a lot of help and guidance when it comes to dealing with and accepting the loss of a loved one.

He helps individuals by educating them with inspirational songs and books that are geared toward bereavement.

My brother uses the book *The Fall of Freddie the Leaf,* by Leo Buscaglia, PhD, to try to help both adults and children understand death and dying. Death and the afterlife are scary and complex thoughts for adults, let alone children.

In this story, Leo talks about the life of a leaf named Freddie. He shows how Freddie makes it through all the seasons and what becomes of him when all the seasons are completed. Leaves all die one day, pretty much at the end of the four seasons. Leaves are guaranteed four seasons starting with spring.

People, on the other hand, aren't guaranteed life from season to season, let alone year to year. When they do pass away many people are left behind to pick up the pieces. Priests are often the people who will help others to get through these trying times and to help them to gradually move on with their lives. He reminds them that it may not be an easy process. Prayer and faith will always be the first step.

Father Steve has watched his own family and friends and many people at the health care center where he lives pass away. It's never an easy situation. He has been there to administer the sacrament of the anointing to these people and to pray with their families. The families at the healthcare facility are all very grateful to have a priest living there who can celebrate Mass and administer the sacraments to their loved ones. Often, at their time of death, they are more than grateful.

My brother has been at a health care facility for eight years now. His nurse will help him cut out the obituaries from the newspaper of people that he knows, and they will hang them all on one wall. Even if he doesn't know the person, but reads about somebody that really concerns him, such as a very young person, he will have it posted. He prays for these people all the time!

Father Steve reading, **The Little Engine That Could,** by Watty Piper at Jacob's kindergarten class seven years ago at the Gesu Catholic School in University Heights, Ohio. His batman shirt was worn under his priest shirt to entertain the children. He was accompanied by Elizabeth, Margie and Mike.

FATHER STEVE'S FAVORITE BLUE ENGINE

I have the strength for everything through him who empowers me.
—Philippians 4:13 (NABRE)

The Little Engine That Could by Watty Piper is a popular children's book loved by not only children but adults. It's a cute little children's story that teaches us a very big lesson. The values of hard work, persistence, and optimism are portrayed in this story about a little blue engine. Just like this little blue engine, Father Steve is constantly encouraged by his passengers on his train of life. I think we've all been on that train where we need help from our friends and encouragement can go a long way. How many times have we gotten strong motivation from one another to be like the little engine to accomplish a task or a goal that we thought was unreachable? It becomes a tough road to travel by ourselves, so we often reach out to others for some inspiration.

These people often fall into our lives at the perfect time, and we often wonder if maybe this was why we met them. After they have helped us, they may leave our lives and move on to someone else like guardian angels reaching out to a person who might be struggling with a situation in their life. Or better yet, they may stay in our lives for the next time that we need them.

My brother's family, friends, doctor, nurses, and physical therapists help his little engine to not only reach the top of the mountain but to continue his journey, just like the little blue engine did. His journey up the mountain, over the top, and down the mountain is filled with a combination of the best of memories and the hardest of times.

God sprinkles joys and celebrations in his life on this journey like something as simple as relaxing with someone enjoying a cup of coffee to baptizing a family member. Special moments include celebrating Mass on Sundays, preaching, and blessing the sick.

Life throws in some very tough times on his journey up, over, and down that mountain. Numerous illnesses, burying friends or family members, the COVID-19 pandemic, and hospital stays are some of the tough times that the journey entails. Persistence and faith are the other two main factors that help him travel up, over, and down that mountain.

One day, my brother asked me if I remembered this story when we were little kids. He asked me over and over again if that little engine ever did make it over the mountain. I told him, yes, it did. I bought the book and read it to him numerous times. I could tell that he was searching for some encouragement. He wanted to go up, go over the mountain, and come down the mountain without any struggles. He just wanted the satisfaction of knowing that he could. I know that deep down inside he wanted to be like that little blue engine. And guess what—he is!

All our lives can be compared to that of that blue engine. We need to remind ourselves a lot of the time through the incentives from others, that we can reach the goals we set for ourselves. Be like the little blue engine who at first said "I think I can," eight times. We can change those four words just like the little blue engine did—to "I thought I could." It's very rewarding to reach our goals knowing that we are like the little blue engine and that we also can make it to the end!

NOT ONE, NOT TWO, BUT THREE TREES

> Then God said: Let the earth bring forth vegetation: every kind of plant that bears seed and every kind of fruit tree on earth that bears fruit with its seed in it. And so it happened: the earth brought forth vegetation: every kind of plant that bears seed and every kind of fruit tree that bears fruit with its seed in it. God saw that it was good.
> —Genesis 1:11–12 (NABRE)

My brother will still enjoy a good children's book and will always pass them on to me. Maybe it's because I was a prekindergarten teacher or maybe it's just because children's books have a simple way of inspiring all of us by using simple words. Some very inspiring words are written very simply and sometimes those are the words that touch our hearts and mean the most to us. It might just be because simple words are easy to remember, and they find a place in our hearts and minds. Sometimes simple words turn into mantras.

The "rule of three" is based on the principle that things that come in threes are inherently funnier, more satisfying, or more effective than any other number. Apparently, it's just how our brain works. Three is the smallest number that can be used to form a distinguishable pattern in our heads. That is why many mantras consist of three words. "God is good" is Father Steve's favorite mantra, and mine is "Happy, Healthy, and Holy." Do you have a daily mantra?

One of his favorite books is *The Tale of Three Trees*, which is written as a traditional folktale. This book uses the number three in its title and is written by Angela Elwell Hunt. Once you find out how the three trees were used, you will realize how these trees have impacted our lives.

Please find the time to pick up this book at your local bookstore, read it, and share it with your family. It's simply a beautiful story for an adult and child to read together. All of them will be inspired by this story. It's a story about three trees on a mountain top who talk to each other about what they want to be when they grow up. Of course, it's an imaginary story, but it is cute for children because we always talk to them about what they want to be when they grow up. Sometimes we as adults still aren't completely grown up and often imagine what we could still do and be in life.

The three trees grow up and end up being used in three remarkable settings. The author tells the reader, "And suddenly the first tree knew he was holding the greatest treasure in the world."

The author continues this amazing story by letting the reader know what happens to the second tree. She tells us, "And suddenly the second tree knew he was carrying the King of heaven and earth."

Lastly, the author lets us know what happens to the third tree. She says, "And every time people thought of the third tree, they would think of God."

This amazing story will inspire you and let you find out what the first tree was holding, what the second tree was carrying and why the third tree would make you think of God. You couldn't possibly imagine or make up this story in your head. It's a very creative story and I had no idea where these three trees would end up.

Thank you, Angela Elwell Hunt, for brightening my day and sending me a little inspiration!

THE INVISIBLE CONNECTION

Faith is the realization of what is hoped for
and evidence of things not seen.
—Hebrews 11:1(NABRE)

My brother received a lot of mail when he was in the hospital. I couldn't wait to read the cards to him because it always brought some happiness to a scary and worrisome day. On a very special day, not only a card, but a package was delivered to his room. The package came from a young girl that my brother knew.

This young girl was twelve and a half years old and needed a tonsillectomy. As most tonsillectomies go without any consequences, she was not one of those lucky ones. After the surgery was performed this young girl began to hemorrhage. The site was repaired, so they thought. Once again, hemorrhaging began. This went on for eleven surgeries. A skin graft was taken from her leg and placed in the area where the bleeding was coming from. This also did not work so a phone call was made to the Pittsburgh Children's Hospital to a specialist. This specialist recommended her to be life flighted immediately to Pittsburgh. The life flight would only take twenty minutes, but her parents had to drive, which would take about two hours. Father Steve, who had been visiting her, stayed with her until the life flight arrived and took off.

She was put into a medically induced comma in the ICU as soon as she arrived. This happened even before her parents arrived. Hopefully, the medically induced coma would allow her throat time to rest and heal. She then needed to be slowly taken off the ventilator to be able to breathe on her own. Father Steve visited her on many occasions and her parents looked forward to his visits as she did. Her mother said that he provided comic relief. He would come in such a good mood that it gave her a break from how bad things were. He came in proudly wearing his Pittsburg Steelers shirts as she proudly wore her Cleveland Browns sweatsuit. Even though they loved different football teams, they both loved Jesus which gave them some common ground. On one occasion, he brought her a pair of rosary beads. These rosary beads were extra special because her throat not only healed, but because they were from an important person in her life who took good spiritual care of her. Her stay in Pittsburgh lasted for two months. After she arrived back home, my brother showed up at her house for a Christmas visit and gathered by the Christmas tree with the family to read, *'Twas the Night Before Christmas,* by Clement Clarke Moore. A special moment indeed!

Inside the package was a letter from the young girl, a book called *The Invisible String,* by Patricia Karst, and a pair of rosary beads. And guess where the rosary beads came from? Yes, they were the same rosary beads that my brother had given her during her illness. She always kept them under her pillow, but now felt that it was time to return these rosary beads to their owner who she felt needed them much more than she did right now. They shared these rosary beads. She had them for twenty years and he has had them for ten years.

Of course, the story about the rosary beads is not over. The rosary beads have an amazing story to them. Father Steve used them often in quiet prayer. One day, a very special day, it was time to turn my brother from side to side to avoid the chance of getting wounds. His rosary beads had somehow fallen behind his back and when they fell, they were spread apart. Since he had been lying on them for two hours, he had an imprint of the rosary on his back. Fifty-nine beads and the cross looked as though they were tattooed on his back. The doctor was called in to see the amazing sight, yet worrisome because the cross and the beads could have caused many little wounds. The doctor even took a picture of my brother's back because he said that he had never seen anything like that before. I didn't know the doctor well enough to ask him to send me the picture because it wasn't his usual doctor. I wish I had the picture to share. They laid him back down as soon as some special cream was applied, so I lost my chance at an unbelievable picture. His skin healed with the cream that they applied. I just looked at him and wondered how and why all these things happened to him and what they all meant.

The book was opened, and I read it to Father. It's an adorable children's story telling us that there is an invisible string that we cannot see that connects all people when we are not together. This is a very soothing story for children that allows them to imagine that their parents are connected to them all day long even when they are not together. It is just like the faith that we have, believing in things that we cannot see!

It is also a great book for adults too. So many of us are going through such tough times and we can't always have people around us, but it is peaceful even for an adult to know that this invisible string somehow can make you feel like you are connected to the ones that you love. When I would leave my brother, he would have that I'm scared look in his eyes. That was the time to remind him that even though I would be an hour's drive from him, our connection was always there, it was just invisible just like the book said. We had some kind of secret gesture that I would do to remind him of it. It seemed so childish, but it worked!

FATHER STEVE'S FAVORITE ADULT BOOKS

> The beginning of wisdom is fear of the Lord, and knowledge of the Holy One is understanding.
> —Proverbs 9:10 (NABRE)

The Bible, of course, is Father's favorite book. He particularly likes the *New American Bible*. His favorite book of the Bible is Psalms because it is a book of praise to God. Father still has his Bible from when he attended Mount St. Mary's Seminary. The binding on his Bible has been duct-taped, which is a true indication that it has been used very often. When you see duct tape on something, you know that it is holding together something that someone won't give up because it is special to them. Well, this definitely holds true in Father Steve's case. He said that if you open the Bible, Psalms will be right in the middle. He likes how the Book of Psalms covers the whole spectrum of emotions. It covers all the ups and downs of what people go through in life.

The Chosen, by Chaim Potok, is definitely a favorite of Father Steve's. He loves to see the interaction between the disciples and how women have a strong role in the book.

The Cross Gardener, by Jason F. Wright, is a great story about how we can find hope by listening and trusting in others. How does someone carry on after a tragedy and who will show them the way? This book tells of a life of a man who lost his daughter and wife in a car accident. He erects two crosses in their honor and one day comes upon someone painting those worn crosses. This person becomes known as the cross gardener. You can follow the life of this man and find out who the cross gardener really is. You will be surprised!

From Cinders to Butterflies: A Spiritual Journey to Healing, written by Richard B. Fratianne, MD. Father Steve met Dr. Fratianne while he was in therapy at Old Brooklyn. Father Steve became friendly with a young man who came to the hospital to work on the hospital beds. This young man was a previous burn victim who was under the care of Dr. Fratianne at one time. Dr. Fratianne helped him to find a reason to want to continue to live despite his burns. This young man was intrigued with Father Steve and saw what he had to deal with every day. Even though my brother wasn't burned, he had daily struggles. The young man encouraged him to speak with the burn doctor and a meeting was set up. Father Steve loved speaking to this doctor and saw how this doctor approached people and reached inside of them to help them find the best in themselves and how to find a reason to keep on going.

No Storm Lasts Forever, by Dr. Terry A. Gordon, a cardiologist. This cardiologist is currently spearheading a national campaign called the Josh Miller HEARTS Act. This will place automated external defibrillators (AEDs) in every school in the country. His book, however, tells the story of his son, Tyler, who sustained a spinal cord injury that left him paralyzed. My sister Elizabeth spoke to Dr. Gordon and was able to set up a meeting with Father Steve and this doctor. The doctor came to the nursing facility to visit my brother and they had a beautiful visit.

Father can truly relate to the book, *Rise and Walk: The Trial and Triumph of Dennis Byrd*, written by Michael D'Orso. Although Dennis Byrd was able to end up walking in his lifetime, the word *paralysis* hit both men in a hard way. Michael's book tells of the trials and tribulations of Dennis Byrd and this book tells of the story of Father Steve. The two men not only had an injury in common, but they were two men who believe in the power of love and faith.

While talking to my brother about his favorite books, he wheeled himself over to the bookshelf and pulled out a book titled, *That Man Is You*, by Louis Evely. I had never heard of the book, but immediately knew that it had to be one of his favorites because the book jacket was about to fall apart. I brought it home and started leafing through it to find a passage that my brother said that he really liked. I got curious about the book because I liked the few things that I read, so it was time to start from the beginning and it was hard to put down.

Louis Evely helps you to put yourself in certain circumstances and delve deep into your heart, mind, and soul and wonder what you would do if you were put in certain situations. He questions you as to what you would have done so many years ago when Jesus was condemned to death. Would you have gone along with all the others who wanted to crucify our Lord, or would you have been the single man to stand up and try to save him? His title, *That Man Is You,* puts you in different settings and lets you really think it through as to how you would handle yourself. A truly empowering book. It's a quick read almost poetic in fashion.

Louis tells, his reader "When we've placed our burden on the only shoulders that can take it, we'll discover that it's light and bearable and that we have what we need to carry it." This is a beautiful way to look at prayer.

Louis reminds us that God speaks to us all the time, "He speaks to us constantly; or, rather, calls us constantly: 'Hello! Don't hang up. I want to talk to you…' And we, are we all ears, breathlessly eager to hear the Lord?"

Lastly, Louis says, "But he talks to us constantly and in his language-one that we don't understand and that we hate to learn: the language of sacrifice and faith and of a prodigiously vast plan to save us, us and the whole world.

Louis has so much to say to us. It was hard not to want to quote everything that he writes. It is just much easier to urge you to read the book.

Father Steve also loves books written by Max Lucado and Sheila Walsh. He couldn't pick a favorite of theirs because he simply just likes their writing and enjoys all their books.

Any book that is written by or about Pope Francis is also a favorite of Father Steve's. He loves that Pope Francis is down to earth and how he relates to everyone.

FATHER STEVE'S FAVORITE SONGS

> Give thanks to the Lord, invoke his name; make known
> among the peoples his deeds! Sing praise to him,
> play music; proclaim all his wondrous deeds!
> —Psalm 105:1–2 (NABRE)

The following are a list and descriptions of my brother's favorite songs. These songs have brought him comfort in the past ten years and have been an important part of his lifelong ministry.

"Amazing Grace," by John Newton, published in 1779. This song was written when John landed safely in Ireland after being caught in a terrible storm at sea. Amazing Grace reflected John's return to faith and the start of his conversion to Christianity.

"Christ, Be Our Light," by Bernadette Farrell. This song is about how Christ takes care of us in all things.

"Holy God, We Praise Thy Name," was written by Ignaz Franz, who was a German Catholic priest, in 1771. This song was our dad's favorite song also. This song tells us to adore God on bended knee.

"Jesus, Take the Wheel," written by Carrie Underwood. This song is about divine intervention in our lives and about letting Jesus help to steer our lives.

"I Am the Bread of Life," by Sister Suzanne Toolan, RSM. This church song is about Christ the Resurrection and what will happen to us if we believe in him.

"Let There Be Peace on Earth," written by Jill Jackson Miller and Sly Miller. This song encourages us to live our lives in peace.

"Rise Again," by Dallas Holm. This is a powerful song about Easter.

"So Much to Thank Him For," by Kevin Spencer. This powerful song makes us think about all the blessings that God bestows on us and how much we should be thankful for them.

"Sunday Is Coming," by Phil Wickham. The song focuses on the life of Jesus, his death, and resurrection. It is a new song that was just released on March 13, 2023.

"The Old Rugged Cross," was written by George Bennard. This artist, a Methodist Evangelist was born in Youngstown, Ohio. A cross has been erected near the pond at the front of Lake Park Cemetery in Youngstown, Ohio. My brother visits there occasionally and spends some time in silent prayer. It is a twenty-two-foot structure set up on the bank of the pond where the cemetery is located with the words "The Old Rugged Cross" engraved on it. George was a Methodist Evangelist, who wrote this country gospel favorite, and seemed to have a vision of Christ on the cross and how they seem inseparable. This song focuses on what Christ had done and sacrificed on the cross at Golgotha, where he died. The date 1913 is engraved on this rock along with the names of the church choir members who were the first to sing this song.

"Walk by Faith," by Marty Haugen. This church song expresses how we walk with faith without seeing or touching the hands of God.

LIFE IN THE NURSING CARE FACILITY

> Then Jesus approached and said to them, "All power in heaven and on earth has been given to me. Go, therefore, and make disciples of all nations, baptizing them in the name of the Father, and of the son, and of the Holy Spirit, teaching them to observe all that I have commanded you. And behold, I am with you always, until the end of the age."
> —Matthew 28:18–20 (NABRE)

> It was time to find a place for my
> brother to live and be at peace.

In the early spring of 2015, we were informed that it was time for us to find a place for Father Steve to live. His rehabilitation time had expired, and it was now time for him to become established into a facility where he would spend the rest of his life.

The search to find the perfect place for my brother to spend the rest of his life took a few weeks because so many places were just not the perfect fit for him. Mike and I visited a few places, and then it was time for my sister and I to go on a few little excursions.

We visited nursing care facilities in Cleveland, Westlake, Akron, Copley, Fairlawn, North Lima, Boardman, and Austintown, Ohio. After checking out a few places, we knew exactly where he shouldn't be and wouldn't want to be. It was time to find the place where we all would want him to be. It was some nice sister time for Elizabeth and me as we drove around, talked a lot, and looked for the perfect and special place that would accommodate our brother.

We revisited places and talked to the administrators, but we needed to find a place that could accommodate his needs, which were many at the time. We eventually found the perfect spot, a place where we felt he would be comfortable, safe, and feel peaceful. He moved into a healthcare facility center in Northeast Ohio on March 17, 2015. It is called Windsor House at Liberty, located in Trumbull County, Ohio.

Mike and I have the opportunity to visit a lot because we are both retired and live less than twenty minutes away. Shortly after Father Steve arrived, we had many teary-eyed visits for all of us. It was time for him to visit the "decision-making tree." My brother had many decisions to make, as we all do. How would he live his life at this facility with some newfound freedom? How would he manage his emotions and keep people in his world? We talked about this tree and how all of us had to make the decision to try to be upbeat no matter the circumstances. We didn't want to be mean people carrying a chip on our shoulders. I understand that everyone has bad days, but we didn't want all our days to be bad. We particularly didn't want to drive away all our friends because we complained all the time. It was time for all of us to find a positive spin on the situation, put God in charge and look forward to some brighter days. And yes, with the help of God, friends, and family brighter days have materialized!

At this nursing facility he receives superb care! All his caregivers are extremely attentive to all his needs and are very respectful of his ministry, making sure that all his concerns are met, especially during a Saturday Mass or prayer service. I never have to worry about whether he is being taken care of or not. I know that he is safe, sound, and secure!

The health-care director, doctor, private duty nurses, facility nurses, aides, and physical therapists look after him constantly and are extremely patient with him when he isn't having a good day. His unhappy face comes out and they all try to put themselves in his shoes, which makes it easier for them to understand what he's dealing with.

How do you find a place that would let you move in, dig up the lawn, and plant two gardens in its place? And who would let you have a polka Mass while celebrating their fall fest? Well, we found that place, and my brother brings them joy just as they all bring him joy.

Father has a private duty nurse with him twenty-four hours a day. They work from 7:00 a.m. to 7:00 p.m. and 7:00 p.m. to 7:00 a.m. They go way beyond their nursing duties. They are not only nurses but have become his true friends. One of his nurses has been with him for seven years. They will pick up oatmeal on their way to work because they know that's what he likes for breakfast. One of them goes thrift store shopping and has come back with some real gems for him. All the time, they're keeping him comfortable and taking care of his needs. They have tons of patience on his not so very good days. They have gotten to know him well and they know when he needs his private prayer time. They deal with mood swings and find various ways and activities to help on days that are difficult for him. They will drive the van and take him to doctor's visits and maybe just go out for a ride on a beautiful day. They watch a lot of TV with him and know about everything happening everywhere since he is a news junkie and watches it all day long when he's in his room. He loves to watch a good basketball or football game so if you aren't a sports fan, you will become one because his sports enthusiasm will get you pumped up too.

The nurses watch over him like a helicopter at times. He must be turned every two hours at night to make sure that he doesn't get any skin breakdowns. If he has a restless night, they try to keep him comfortable. Since his body temperature cannot be regulated because of his paralysis, the nurses always must deal with him either being too cold or too hot. They do various things to try and accommodate him. They follow him on hospital visits and even stay there with him. They learn all about his ministry, and if they don't understand things, they will ask him. If they don't know Jesus before they meet him, they will know Jesus real soon. If he is having any kind of service for his ministry, they'll go out of their way to make sure he has everything he needs.

My brother has been known to wheel around the facility distributing Easter candy, holy cards, and palm crosses. The palm crosses are made from wood, and they fit perfectly into the palm of your hand, giving them the name palm cross. They are great prayer crosses for people who especially like to hold on to something. People love these little trinkets that deal with faith or Jesus because they see a man faced with adversity that won't give up on God. This gives them strength to deal with their weaknesses. At Christmas, he drove around distributing coffee mugs that his nurse picked up for him filled with cocoa and marshmallows to celebrate the Christmas season. He passed them to some of the workers in the center. He'll decorate the entranceway of the facility with Christmas trees and a large Nativity scene.

Father Steve celebrating Christmas Mass
at Liberty Healthcare Center.

The private duty nurses keep in touch with me all the time to let me know what is going on if I am not at the facility. These nurses have become like a part of our family!

Father Steve's life went from a loud big world to a quiet and small world. He now has one room compared to a rectory like where he used to live. Everyone has made his room cozy and comfortable for him. It's hard for him to plan ahead for any company when he really doesn't know how he'll be feeling on that day. Sometimes the phone call with someone just checking up on him is enough to fulfill his day. Cards, gifts, and messages have all been appreciated by him and all of us more than people realize.

Father Steve has two favorite prayers that he prays daily, morning and night. These two prayers remind Father Steve daily that he is called to be an instrument of peace and to daily practice wisdom to know what he can and cannot change in his life.

"The Prayer of St. Francis" is believed to have been written by Father Esther Bouquerel. The Great War of 1916 made this a prayer for the tough times. The prayer tells us that we should spread God's word of peace to everyone.

"The Serenity Prayer," was written by Reinhold Niebuhr. This is an extremely powerful prayer telling us to learn the difference between what we can and cannot change in our lives. There comes a time when we must understand this difference and figure out what we will do about it. After my brother performed the marriage ceremony for a special couple, the wife cross-stitched "The Serenity Prayer," which she framed and now hangs on Father Steve's wall near his door. This framed prayer reminds him daily as he passes through his room to accept his life because only God has the power to change it.

He begins his day with these prayers. Next, he will have the nurse put a chain around his neck consisting of his dad's dog tags. On the same chain, there is a cross and a ring that has the "Our Father" written on it. He requests a cup of coffee and the newspaper from his private duty nurse. He cannot make his own cup of coffee. Even if he could get out of bed to make the coffee, the task would be so unsafe. Yes, a Keurig coffee maker makes coffee quickly, but he would have to grab that coffee cup ever so carefully not to burn himself. Even if he could make that cup of coffee, he can't even get out of bed without the help of two people and a slide board or a Hoyer lift that would be used. This couldn't even happen for a few hours because he must wait until there are two people to help him with the task. He'll enjoy that cup of coffee made by the nurse, read the morning paper, and he'll listen to music on his iPad with a great variety of genres. Maybe he'll finish reading a good book or use his phone for some communication. Before he knows it, it's high noon and lunch will arrive and he'll need to get out of bed, get dressed and go to therapy.

My brother goes to physical therapy five days a week and the therapy room is located very close to his room. As he enters or exits the therapy room, he passes by a very large peace lily in the foyer and passes by the concierge. Between the peace lily and the concierge, he embraces a sense of peace inside his heart because the concierge too looks after him any time that she can with her peaceful, sweet, and caring disposition. She joined the helicopter brigade as another one keeping their eye on him. He has a whole host of angels watching over him at this facility. You won't find another one like it!

The room is surrounded by huge windows that bring in a lot of light and it's a great place to be, especially when the weather outside is sunny. There is a guardian angel on the wall which overlooks the patients. The feast day of the Guardian Angel is October 2. My brother said that he remembers back when we went to Catholic school and in grade school, we were taught by the nuns who taught us to always scoot over on our seat and leave a little place for our Guardian Angel. My brother feels comforted by this angel as he exercises to get restored back to good health. He can ride the recumbent bike until he gets tired and he almost triumphs to beat his time or pace from the day before. The bike will record much of the activity his legs are doing compared to the help of the bike. The recumbent bike is a stationary piece of equipment that is easy on the patient's joints. It improves cardiovascular fitness and promotes muscle strength and helps to restore your range of motion. He loves sitting there riding his bike. Arm exercises will follow with Father Steve using five-or-eight-pound weights. There's a basketball hoop in the room where he will either play basketball during therapy or when company comes to visit. Sometimes he'll simply just play catch using the ball. He has a wheelchair that can enable him to stand up. There are straps that go across his chest that hold him upright and a device that goes across his knees to stabilize them. My brother can then converse with people face to face. After therapy, my brother may go for a ride or spend time reading and listening to music. Being the news junkie that he is, the news station will be on.

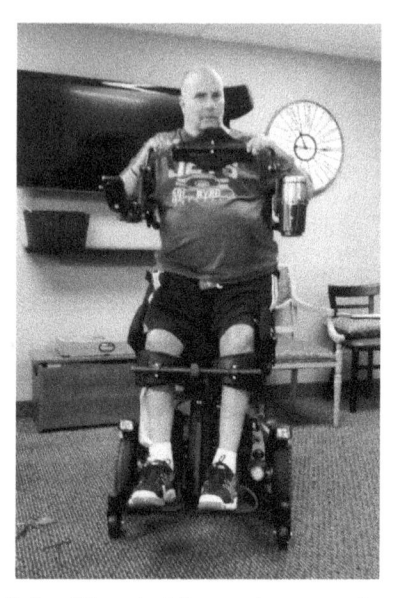

Father Steve building endurance using his standing-up wheelchair.

For the first four and a half years that Father Steve lived at this facility, he was able to have the celebration of Mass every Saturday in the activity room. Patients, family, friends, coworkers and families of the patients attended every week. Different people would be there every Saturday, except for the dedicated ones who showed up every Saturday to help with Mass.

He began with a makeshift altar since that was all we had to work with. A friend of my husband, who is a carpenter, was able to design an absolutely gorgeous altar for him, one that he was able to ride his wheelchair under. He was able to sit comfortably under the altar and be able to reach his chalice, ciborium, book or whatever he needed. A special cross that was purchased by a friend was placed in the front in the center of the altar. Nothing else was placed on the altar except an altar cloth with a relic in it. Everybody at the center respected this altar and when Mass was over the altar was moved aside and covered up and no one ever touched it. One of the activity aids would print out music sheets every week for all of us to join in the singing. She would do her homework and look up the correct music that would be sung to match the readings of that Saturday. Sometimes, my brother had stories or prayers that were printed out and passed out to all who attended. I was the Eucharistic Minister, which was an honor. He is now forever grateful for the Eucharistic ministers who bring him communion. Mike was the Mass server for Father Steve. If there was a time when we couldn't be there, numerous friends would take over. During the Lenten season, a purple cloth was spread out in front of the altar. For the Lenten season, I would decorate with rocks and branches and pussy willows. On Palm Sunday, blessed palms were distributed to anyone who attended Mass and to whoever wanted them that lived in the facility. On one Palm Sunday occasion, our brother, John, from California sent my brother palms from his state. That made it a special Palm Sunday for us, feeling that our brother from California was right there with us. For Easter, a fountain was strategically placed next to the altar and a special couple would go out and buy lilies, daffodils, hyacinths and tulips to be placed in front of the altar. It was always bought with their own money. What great friends! A gorgeous advent wreath that was decorated with evergreen foliage was placed near the altar during the Advent season. During Christmas, these same friends would go out and buy poinsettias that were placed in front of the altar on a white cloth. It was a Saturday that we all looked forward to at four o'clock. Oftentimes, we would all gather and have a picnic in the area outside the activity room where we had a grill and were able to cook out. Everybody brought something to these picnics. If we didn't have a picnic, we might have gone out to eat. It was perfect!

It was a wonderful special time for all involved and we had a great spiritual and friendly connection. It was almost like having a little spiritual club that we all belonged to. We watched a priest who gave up riding a motorcycle to now riding a wheelchair and watched how he never questioned God why this happened to his life. It kind of made us stop questioning the petty things that happen in our lives.

Unfortunately, all this came to an abrupt stop with the COVID-19 pandemic!

Yes, the COVID-19 pandemic changed the lives of many people. Mass had to be halted for a long time. A simple prayer service was offered for a few of the residents. While attending my brother's prayer service, I looked around the room and noticed all the changes that the pandemic caused. His Saturday Mass with attendance of about twenty residents and twenty laypeople dwindled down to maybe eight residents and four laypeople. Outsiders were not encouraged to come because of the virus. His big beautiful altar was now a simple table, maybe twelve inches by twelve inches. There was a cross and an angel placed on the table. A colored fabric that correlated with the color of the church season hung from the podium where a reader could stand to read a reading.

As I sat there and observed what was going on, I became teary-eyed to see how small my brother's world had become. I missed all the other residents and the friends, relatives, and parishioners that would come from all the previous parishes where my brother had formerly worked. I did a reading, said some prayers, and sang a song. Later on in the week, I spoke to a woman from a religious order and told her my thoughts about my brother's new world. She looked at me sincerely; and with a soft, convincing voice, she told me that God doesn't always work with big numbers and doesn't necessarily like big numbers. In the book of Matthew, God tells us, "For where two or three are gathered together in my name, there am I in the midst of them." She made it a point for me to understand that if my brother only saved a few souls from where he lives, he will have done his job. It made me think about the story *The Star Thrower*, by Loren Eiseley.

This story tells about a little boy who walks up and down the beach, throwing starfish that the tide brought in back into the water. An older man approaches him and tells the little boy that he is pretty much wasting his time because he'll never get to take care of all the starfish that are washed ashore. The little boy throws in one more, looks at the man, and says, "I made a difference to that one."

So there I thought, *He'll make a difference to a few souls that he may save now, not a huge number of souls, like he did in the past.* It also reminded me of the parable of the good shepherd, where God is the shepherd and leaves ninety-nine sheep to go and find the one that was lost. He is the God who searches for that stray person and brings them back. I thought about God, numbers, and how many, many years ago, he only picked twelve disciples to teach and heal. He didn't pick hundreds or thousands. My brother's small world and small numbers started to make sense. It's all good now.

Now, back to my brother's schedule. The night nurse comes at 7:00 p.m. and stays until 7:00 a.m. Sometimes he has a very restful and peaceful night falling asleep to the sound of rain on his iPad or religious music. After a good night's rest, he'll get up early in the morning, but if he has a restless night, he'll sleep in the next day. Sometimes, he's very pleasant and happy and at other times mood swings take over making some days long and dreary and just not good. On a bad day, I always try to remind him that tomorrow will be completely different. A lesson can be learned even on the worst of days, and this is where his faith comes into play. He spends ninety percent of his day depending on people for pretty much everything. My days are not anything like that and I bet yours aren't either!

The spinal cord injury patient has a whole life adjustment. When a patient leaves a spinal cord hospital the doctors and nurses tell them that all they need to do is make some adjustments to their life and they'll be okay. Some things can be adjusted, but many cannot. I don't know how you adjust your lifestyle after you've been riding a motorcycle, participating in a polar plunge, swimming in the ocean, or lying on a beach somewhere. I'm not sure how you make all these new adjustments. I guess you just need to focus your life on many other activities and come to the realization that it may be a time to discover a new interest or hobby.

Apparently, it's easy for a person to say just go home and make a few adjustments when they're standing and not sitting in a wheelchair like you may be. I'm sure they all mean well, but it's a tough road out there when you get out there. Sometimes I wonder if a healthcare worker would just spend one day in a wheelchair and one night as a spinal cord patient, their advice might be a little bit different to the patients when they leave the hospital.

The amount of patience that a spinal cord patient must have can't possibly compare to the patience that you or I need to get through the day. They're pretty much dependent on everyone for everything. They're pretty much a prisoner in their own body some days. Their life will most definitely depend on what they decide to do with that prisoner. On the days when Father Steve feels like this, it would be a good time for him to reflect on the encouragement that he would give to the prisoners he once visited. He needed to accept the advice he once gave out which might be an extra boost that he needed. He is the only person who knows how he feels, and he is the only person who can change his feelings and outlook on life.

Father Steve would not be alive today if it wasn't for the amazing nursing care that the director of the facility where he lives makes sure that he gets, along with his private duty nurses!

Father Steve relaxing in his room enjoying the peace and quiet and his relative's artwork on his wall.

Father Steve relaxing and enjoying some fresh air outside his facility.

REMINISCING WITH MY BROTHER

> Rejoice always. Pray without ceasing. In all circumstances give thanks, for this is the will of God for you in Christ Jesus.
> —1 Thessalonians 5:16–18 (NABRE)

My brother and I discussed how we wouldn't be the people that we are today, if it wasn't for the people that have entered our lives. And what about all the people that have entered our lives for a short time and have left? We also are the people we are today because of what happened in our past. Our past defines us now.

Just a few weeks ago, we went to the movie called *His Only Son*. It is the Bible story of Abraham and Rebecca. Abraham was asked by God to sacrifice his only son in a ceremony. Abraham was willing to do this because of his love and devotion that he had to God. In this movie, Abraham is reminded by God that he will have descendants as many as there are stars in the sky. At night, my brother can see the stars that light up on his ceiling and be reminded of this story, and it confirms the faith and love that he too has for the Lord, just as Abraham did.

Lately, I drove past some church signs that made me want to go hmm. They shared with motorists the following messages, which I shared with my brother:

> Choose the Bread of Life, or you are toast.
> When you are down to nothing, God is up to something.
> Don't tell God about the big storm; tell
> the storm about your big God.
> If you walk with the Lord, you'll never be out of step.

When life isn't a bed of roses, remember who wore the thorns
Honk if you love Jesus, text while driving if you want to meet him.
Having trouble sleeping? Don't count sheep; talk to the Shepherd.
Swallowing pride will never give you indigestion.
Weather forecast: God reigns; the sun shines.
Be an organ donor and give your heart to Jesus.
God isn't calling us to go to church; he's calling us to be his church.
If you are more fortunate than others, build
a longer table not a taller fence.
Store the Bible in your heart, not on a shelf.

As my brother and I sat and reminisced the other day about some of the times in our lives, my brother looked at me and started talking about the days when we used to play the flutophone, now called the recorder, in grade school. After the school year was about to end, students were gathered for a recital. My brother would sit on the balcony watching the director of all the grade school children as they gathered for the big recital. He said that one day he wanted to be that director. Well, my brother grew up and entered the priest ministry where he helps people find comfort in their lives if they were troubled. He gives them some direction, but he knows that God is the true director of our lives just like the director oversees his symphony.

We talked about our lives too and how it can be compared to the heartbeat printout that you get from the doctor's office after you have had an EKG. All the ups and downs that you see on the printout are like the ups and downs in our life. It is up to us to decide what we will do with the downs because we all like the ups. But what do we do with those downs? It might be time to put God in charge!

As my brother and I sat outside on a sunny day, he stared talking about minus and plus signs. I couldn't figure out where he was heading with this conversation. It almost sounded like a math lesson. He continued to explain there are many minus signs in our lives but only one plus sign. Father Steve explained to me that the minus signs are the constant hardships that we endure throughout life. The minus signs could be an illness; divorce; miscarriage; losing a spouse, child, or dear one; losing your job; or simply just dealing with a bad day. While we are experiencing these minus signs, we need to look at the big picture and picture the cross that Jesus hung on. That is the plus sign that we should never forget. It reminds us of how Jesus suffered for us but was resurrected. It should remind us that one day we, too, will join Jesus in heaven. On our minus-sign days, it is important for us to keep the image of the cross in our minds to remind us of eternal life.

We continued to talk about life in general and my brother reminded me that life is almost like a soda machine. Sometimes you get what you press for or pray for, and sometimes you don't get what you press for or pray for. You might put your money in the machine, press the button for the Diet Coke and Diet Coke comes out of the machine. Of course, you are pleased. The next time you are at the soda machine you put your money in, press the button for your Diet Coke, but out comes Barq's Root Beer. You're disappointed that you didn't get the Diet Coke, but the Barq's Root Beer is going to be okay. You at least got something. Maybe the machine just malfunctioned, or something just went haywire. What happens the next time when you put your money in, press the Diet Coke button, and out comes nothing, not even a Barq's Root Beer? What made it even worse was that you didn't even get your money back. How disappointing is that? You probably won't want to use that soda machine again. Somehow you feel like you got cheated.

This analogy is kind of like when your grandma is sick, and her outlook is not good. You pray for Grandma to be totally healed and she is. This outcome is great, and you are very pleased about Grandma and, of course, God. Poor Grandma gets sick once again, so you pray for Grandma's good health. This time, Grandma recovered; however, she is just okay. You are not totally pleased about Grandma, but you still have Grandma, so you'll take Grandma this way. God answered your prayers; not totally, but his way. But what happens the next time Grandma gets sick, and she doesn't make it after you have prayed and prayed and prayed? Do you now feel that God did not answer your prayers? Do you now feel like you were cheated?!

Well, I guess life is really like the soda machine. It's hard to compare Diet Coke to Grandma, but sometimes things in life, little or big, are disappointing, and you need to decide what to do with the outcome. Your prayer was not answered the way that you expected, but as my brother has said many times, "God doesn't always answer our prayers, but enables us to live with the questions." Maybe let God in, and you just might find what you are looking for! We all might have to live with those questions if we didn't get the answers we expected.

So I just went to the snack vending machine for Father Steve the other day. I put in $1.05 for a bag of chips and $1.05 for a bag of pretzels. Well, I guess I hit the jackpot because out came two bags of chips and two bags of pretzels. I got twice as much for what I paid for. I guess that's like a day when God blesses you with way more than what you expected or even prayed for.

God also gives all of us the prize package of eternal life. We will all hit the jackpot one day!

THE ROAD OF LIFE

Help me, Lord my God; save me in your mercy.
—Psalm 109:26 (NABRE)

Just like the road you drive your car on, the road of life has very similar aspects. On your road of life, you'll encounter smooth roads, speed bumps, speed limits, curves, turns, holes, detours, and stop signs. Gosh, every one of those sounds like something you might feel you can tackle on the road, but you wouldn't want to tackle in life.

Smooth Roads

The smooth road is the easy one. We all enjoy traveling on this road. We get to where we want to go on time because there is nothing on the road that will prevent that from happening. This road puts smiles on our faces.

We also love the smooth road of life. This smooth road of life means that we'll have a pleasant day—most likely, a pretty darn perfect day. Our day at work goes very smoothly, and we might even be offered a promotion. Our children all come home saying that they had a great day in school, and one of them may have even been given an award. We cook supper, it turns out great, and our whole family just wants to stay home for the evening, play some board games, or just relax together because after all, it's been a picture-perfect day!

The smooth road for Father Steve begins with his morning cup of coffee and newspaper. The morning could start very early or may not start out until high noon, but that means it's a good one. His transfer out of bed goes smoothly and he'll pick out his outfit for the day. If it's football or basketball season he'll be proud to sport a YSU,

Pittsburgh Steelers, San Antonio Spurs, or a Georgia Bulldog shirt. If he's in a country Western mood, his chest may be adorned with a Willie Nelson, Vince Gill, or Nashville T-shirt. One of his favorites is his lifeguard shirt, maybe because he was a lifeguard way back when. This is a different kind of lifeguard shirt than you would expect. The shirt is bright red with a cross in the center of it. On either side of the cross are the words *Jesus Christ*. The words "My Lifeguard Walks on Water," encompasses the cross. Another one of his favorite shirts would be the shirt with *The Chosen* written on it which stands for the movie and book which Father Steve loves. Mealtime, physical therapy, and nighttime all go smoothly, giving him a good night's rest.

Speed Bumps

If you travel too fast over speed bumps on the road, your vehicle can suffer. You can have trouble with the wheel alignment, springs, shocks, or the speed bump can even cause the tire to blow. Speed bumps are traffic-calming devices. They help to slow down motor vehicle traffic. Speed bumps in life can be a good thing.

Do you ever have days when you run and run and run around? A good life speed bump will make us slow down whether we want to or not. The speed bump might be a phone call from someone who needs us, or we may have an "I don't feel too good moment" when we decide to take a break and rest. Most of the time, it's a much-needed rest, so the speed bump is a very good thing.

On days when my brother is feeling great, he tends to want to go and go and go. Yes, I get it. He's feeling good, and the first two letters of *good* spell *go*, and that's what he wants to do. A good speed bump will slow him down, rest his body, and help him get refueled for the rest of the day. A good speed bump is just time telling him to take a welcomed break that he didn't realize he may have needed. A speed bump can slow my brother down enough that a good night's rest will be in order.

Speed Limits

Speed limits are posted on the streets and highways to keep motor vehicles from either going too fast or too slow. You will find out very quickly if you disobey that speed limit sign when you see flashing lights following you.

If there was a posted speed limit in our life, and it was seventy miles per hour, we would be in a hurry, literally going fast and probably multitasking. We would be feeling great and almost feeling free, going full speed ahead! When we are not feeling well, the twenty-mile-per-hour school speed zone is welcomed in our life. It gives us time to relax and refresh!

For Father Steve, a seventy-mile-per-hour speed limit would be an over-the-top day. This sometimes would almost be too much for him as he usually would prefer the twenty-mile-per-hour school zone speed limit day. He doesn't like to be rushed as many of us would agree. The twenty-mile-per-hour speed limit suits him just fine. He likes a relaxing day, limited stress, soft music, and peace and quiet. He'll often ask me why everyone seems so loud and moving and talking so fast. I told him that his world was once like that too, loud and fast! The twenty-mile-per-hour speed limit helps him to have relaxing meals and helps him to drift off to sleep.

Curves and Turns

The curves and turns on the road give us a chance to maybe turn in a different direction than the path we planned. We may turn the wrong way and find something completely different on our path, something we never expected.

Sometimes, curves or turns in life make us better people. We may be forced to turn our life around and try new experiences, maybe even find things that we never thought we would like. This new adventure may result in a whole new lifestyle for us and open our eyes to a wonderful new world. And just think of the people that we will meet by taking a different turn in our life.

My brother's curves and turns in his life have brought different people into his life. Every time he turns the corner he meets a new doctor, nurse, physical therapist, or another stranger. How these people have impacted his life cannot be measured in any way. They show him so much compassion, kindness, and care. They help him to manage his new life, and in turn, they can say that they met a faithful individual who just won't give up. It's a good situation for everyone. A curve or a turn might send him to a new restaurant that he hasn't tried yet and maybe a change in the music that helps him to fall asleep.

Holes in the Road

Holes in the road are so irritating to come upon. You can end up with a flat tire, missing hubcap, or a bent rim.

Hitting a hole in the road of life almost feels like we bent our rim, are missing a hubcap, or maybe even feel like we have a flat tire. It shocks and often stuns us. Something unexpected pops up like a sickness or a bill. Maybe it's the car insurance statement or house taxes. We knew it was coming in the mail; we just weren't sure when the mailman would put that hole in our day. They always say "Don't hate the messenger," because, come on, we knew it was coming. We just didn't feel like falling in the hole when our day was going so well. But who does?

Father Steve's holes in the road have often resulted in surgeries, hospital stays, and UTIs leaving him septic. The COVID-19 pandemic not only left a hole in the road of life, but just about left an earthquake in people's lives. The COVID-19 pandemic put visitation at nursing homes on hold, causing a strain on people's families and friends. The nursing facility where my brother lives followed all the guidelines that they were given and never made any exceptions. Patients were confined to their rooms for probably the first two years the virus was active. No food was permitted to be brought in from restaurants or any of our own home-cooked meals for over a year. After that, groceries were permitted, but needed to be disinfected by the staff. The safety of the patients was the goal of the nursing home, and I had to agree with that. Lots of phone calls and window visits were permitted. My brother fared well through all this and did what he had to do and didn't do anything that would jeopardize his health. As the Holy Spirit sits at his door, my brother still has not caught the virus. He can get out freely now but goes out cautiously. A hole in the road for him could simply mean that pickle they accidentally put on his sandwich or a night of continually waking up.

Detours on the Road

But what about the infamous detour on the road? Detours are welcomed by no one, but at least the detour on the road is posted. When we come upon a detour on the road, it sends us on a new path. Hopefully, a detour route is posted for us to follow. We might like this detour that takes us on different roads through different neighborhoods. Sometimes that detour takes us on a route way out of our way. We are probably going to be late for our destination, unless we are those prepared people who leave their house in anticipation of a hiccup in the road.

We often don't find the detour in our life posted anywhere until it's too late. On the road, we might not have enough time to pick another path, or we can't find another path that would make us happy. The detours in our life are like those on the road. We may have to change our path in life because of a sudden unexpected scenario or tragedy. Our life can quickly change because this unexpected event makes us change our plans. Sometimes these unexpected changes of plans turn out to be better plans and are a good change for our lives.

On November 13, 2013, Father Steve was sent on the detour of his life. He had to find a new way to do everything that everyone else takes for granted. He'll never be able to perform certain tasks again. This detour put him in what is called a "new normal." He spends every day and night figuring out this "new normal." Eating and sleeping habits have all been changed because of this new way of life.

The Stop Sign

That octagon-shaped red-and-white stop sign demanding that we stop at once is often unexpected on the road.

Sometimes in life, we must stop abruptly just as if someone planted that stop sign right in our face. It might appear unexpectedly, or we might see or feel that stop sign in our life coming toward us. It is usually never welcomed, unless of course that stop sign comes with some good news attached to it. We might have to stop for a casualty, or maybe we will be asked to stop immediately to hear the best news of our lives.

Father Steve has seen that octagon-shaped red-and-white stop sign frequently during the last ten years. It has interfered with physical therapy, eating, and sleeping. Father Steve courageously stops, does what he must do, and plows right through it.

It's so easy to accept the smooth roads of life. Occasional speed bumps and changes in the speed limit in our lives help to keep us on our toes and to pay attention to what we're doing. Curves and turns in our life usually aren't all that bad. Now the holes in the road, the detours, or the abrupt stop will probably become a challenge.

Once again, we see the decision-making tree. Sometimes we may need help from other people on how to make the proper decision. Maybe it's because we're young or maybe just inexperienced. Maybe we are at a time in our life when we feel burned out and can't even mentally wrap our heads around a decision that might affect the rest of our lives. We may need the advice of family or friends to help us plow through it. Since our decision will be the final say so, a call out to God should be in order.

YES, GOD REALLY IS GOOD!

> Merciful and gracious is the Lord, slow
> to anger, abounding in mercy.
> —Psalm 103:8 (NABRE)

Besides my all-time favorite Christmas song, "O Holy Night," my favorite song from the '70s is "Landslide," by Fleetwood Mac. I like the main singer of the song, Stevie Nicks, and the melody. I've had a great life, so the lyrics of the song have nothing to do with how I lived the first sixty years of my life. The last ten years, however, could have been like that of a landslide. A landslide refers to the downhill movement of rocks, soil, or debris. My brother's surgeries, doctor visits, procedures, cultures, blood work, sleepless nights, bad news, X-rays, and swallow tests, just to name a few, were like the rocks, soil and debris in my life. Was my life like a massive movement of prayer, hard work, family and friends that was slowly moving away from me?

Sitting down to relax, I looked at my husband and said that I couldn't believe that I was turning seventy years old in June. Where were my sixties, and what happened to the last decade of my life? It took a little while to wrap my head around it all. After a little discussion with Mike and a cup of coffee, I realized that the last decade of my life was spent focusing a good part of my life on the needs of my brother.

The flipside of that is that he fulfilled my needs even more. How do you watch your brother that you grew up with struggle through life and hope that you are doing enough for him? I dislike the words *I could have, I should have,* and *I would have,* and I felt that I never wanted to say them. I felt like the pressure was on me, but in reality, the pressure was on my brother even more. He had the part of being the role model to me and everyone else. It was his job to follow all the moral and ethical codes of his religion and show to me and everyone else that his faithfulness to God meant steady loyalty and trusting in him with your whole body, mind, and soul.

So the decade of my life was spent watching my sibling be strong and patient while he encouraged me to be the same. There were many tears from him and me along the way. At times I produced some very inspiring words to encourage him on a bad day. I thought that I came up with those words all by myself, but I truly knew the Holy Spirit was behind me the whole time. The seven gifts of the Holy Spirit are wisdom, understanding, counsel, fortitude, knowledge, piety, and fear of the Lord. He was truly working through me with the gifts of wisdom and understanding, while my brother practiced the Holy Spirit's gift of fortitude.

I now finally see some peace and comfort in my brother's eyes, a change from the many years before. Maybe it would finally be time for me to find that peace too. Being frustrated was so exhausting. I didn't want to be mad at God. He's been so very good to me and my family. They say things happen for a reason. We will all find out the reason for this tragedy and all the tragedies that people have endured because God promises us that it will all make sense one day!

I did lots and lots of praying in different places, at different times, and in different ways. I prayed at home, in church, while walking along the beach, walking in the snow, traveling in the car, and pretty much wherever the day would take me. I prayed in the morning, during the day, and even during the night. I prayed using prayer books and rosary beads, and I made up my own prayers. After continually praying and a lot of soul searching, I finally found in my heart a special place that truly let me know that yes, God is good! I realized that for God to be considered good he didn't have to help my brother by making him walk. So yes, I did see a miracle happen. No, my brother is not walking, but it truly is a miracle that we have all made it through the last ten years. What makes God so good is how he did and does take care of us and gets us through our daily struggles, heartaches, hardships, pains, and life tragedies. We may not all be healed here on earth, but God will always carry us as the "Footprints in the Sand," poem reminds us. God does have our backs. It took me years to really realize this, and it might take you some time too, but that's okay.

I didn't lose those ten years of my life, but instead during those ten years, I have gained and embraced a wonderful and peaceful relationship with the Lord that would have never happened otherwise. I have met the most unique people who have enriched my life and who have taught me important lessons about life and myself that I couldn't see on my own. People are amazing!

We all wonder what our purpose in life really is. For some people, it comes easily; and for others, they may pass away without having figured it out.

I believe now that my purpose in life is to simply spread my faith to my family and to write this book about a faith-filled family to share with all of you. If I can reach many people with this book about faith, it would be wonderful. If I can only reach one person, then I am fine with that too. If you love Jesus, then you'll love this book. If you like Jesus, then you may find a reason in this book to start loving him. If you are simply not a follower of Jesus, then hopefully, I may have helped you see Jesus in a different light. I wrote this book because I felt that I owed it to my brother to share his story and show people how they should embrace their lives and all their blessings. Remember you are not lucky, you are blessed! I want people to see how faith and determination can take you to another level in your life. I want people to understand how precious life really is. I feel that I owed this book to God too because he has blessed me so abundantly and I needed to share my story about faith to all of you. I wanted to share with everyone how God has taken my brother and my family on an unbelievable journey and how he has never left our sides. I wrote this book using notebook paper and six pencils. They are all now only a few inches long. One is for me to keep forever, and my five grandchildren will each get a pencil that their grandmother used to write a book about faith as a memento.

I finished writing this book and decided to put it in God's hands to see if he wanted it to be published or not. It would be up to him! So if you are reading this book, then yes, God wanted this story about a simple faith-filled man and the journey that he spends with Father Steve to be shared with all of you!

After writing this book, I feel like a load has been taken off my shoulders. I look at life differently and so much more appreciative of every morning that is ahead of me. I will always love and remember the good faithful memories of the last decade, but now, I will totally practice mindfulness and enjoy the time we all have together and focus on what the future will hold for us instead of always reliving the hard times from the last decade of my life.

The last ten years of my life was just spent with a man engulfed in the Lord. He looked at me before one of his last procedures and just said, "Let's see what the Lord does with this one." No matter the circumstances, Father Steve has always put his life in the hands of the Lord. Now isn't that a wonderful place to put your life?

I've learned from my brother that life is so much easier when the hands of the Lord are engulfed around you. Once again, Father Steve told me that God doesn't give us the answers to our questions, he enables us to live with the questions!

So what about the title of my book, *Have You Seen my Brother?* When I began to share my book with my son Mikey, he asked me what I would title my book and why. He looked at me inquisitively when I told him the title and he quickly encouraged an explanation from me. I promptly explained to him that I felt as though I often don't know or recognize the man that everyone has called my brother in the last ten years. My brother looked and acted so differently. In my heart, I really truly wondered if anyone had seen him because I couldn't find him. Mikey said that he did indeed like my title.

I explained to Mikey that my brother and I spent a lot of time with our parents and siblings and were together on all holidays while we grew up. We always had the best of times. After I married my husband and had my children, the fun times continued. We spent quite a bit of time with Father Steve. We played on the slip and slide, fished around his lake, and shot off fireworks on the Fourth of July. We went to picnics, sporting events, out to eat, festivals, church events and services, or simply went out for ice cream. There were too many fun times to mention. It was a guarantee that you would have fun if you were with Father Steve.

I watched my brother and how he handled other people during the tough times in their lives. I watched from a distance and sometimes I watched close by how he took care of people in need and people during tragedies. I watched him visit the sick and watched how he handled my parents at the end of their lives. He always appeared so very strong and almost invincible. I thought and hoped that I would never see my brother on the other end of a tragedy.

After thinking about my title, Mikey, without even thinking twice looked at me and said, "Mom, he's been there right in front of you the whole time. You just never saw him under those circumstances." Wow, now I finally had the clarity that I needed. I guess I needed someone to point that out and who better than a family member, my son, who has known me for almost forty-four years. Father Steve was always pictured in my head as the fun brother that spent many of his days with the sick and dying. I just couldn't picture him on the other end of the spectrum in those conditions, and I guess I honestly didn't want to. But who would? I now saw him at the other end of tragedy.

So yes, I did find my brother! He was right there in front of me the whole time; he wasn't lost at all. Maybe I was the one who was lost at times. I sure did spend a lot of time looking for God and my brother. Maybe they were hanging out together the whole time. So I not only found my brother, but I found a good God who was there the whole time too, so it was a win-win situation for me.

I finally saw the strong and powerful brother that was with me the last ten years. His past four-hundred-pound bench press of weight pushing up into the air now means nothing compared to the amount of faith that I see him bench press up to God!

If God was a genie and gave me three wishes, I would have asked for so many different things throughout my lifetime. When I look back, those three wishes that I would have chosen would have gotten me nowhere in life and seem so trivial now. My three wishes for me and my family wouldn't be three wishes, but simply just three words… a peaceful life!

It was now time to change my favorite song from "Landslide," by Fleetwood Mac to, "What a Wonderful World," by Louis Armstrong. Yes, my life truly is a wonderful world!

A tattoo of "God is Good" intermingled with a cross and a sunflower, for warmth, now rests on my ankle. It reminds me that with every step I take the rest of my life, I am constantly reminded that God is with me and how good he really is!

There are 3,600 seconds in an hour. It would be wonderful if all of us would spend just a few of those seconds each day remembering the three favorite words of Father Steve:

GOD IS GOOD!

EPILOGUE

Goodbye

Father Steve is described as quirky, totally unpredictable, and extremely generous with his heart and wallet. He was the most faith-filled person that I have ever met. He gave it his all till the very end and fought a very hard battle never losing his ministry. He was the epitome of faith and perseverance. It was never about him, but all of us around him. He was on this pilgrimage with his family and every one of you. Most importantly, he is described as a man of God who was so very proud and excited about being a priest. God and his faith were always number one and no one or nothing on this earth could change that. He reminded me every day that God is good whether he was having a good day or lying in a hospital bed. He was the best of the best!

With a drastic turn of events, the following paragraphs give a different ending to my book.

I lost my brother and one of my very best friends on January 14, 2024, at 2:48 p.m. Somehow, I knew that it would be on a Sunday, the day on which he spent so many years celebrating Mass.

The last ten years have been hard and trying, but his final twelve days that we spent with him in the hospital were even harder, consisting of a lot of drama and uncertainty. He entered the hospital on January 3, 2024, after a COVID-19 positive test which left him with some respiratory issues. I knew that the positive test results would be a tough diagnosis for him to fight through. He was soon labeled a complex patient with numerous medical issues going on. Every single day either started with or ended with a new problem. The staff at St. Elizabeth hospital in downtown Youngstown were beyond amazing, showing medical expertise with a lot of empathy toward my brother and our entire family. They respected my brother as being a priest and their greeting when they entered the room was no longer Mr. Popovich, but Father.

Medical decisions needed to be made between my sister, Liz and myself and we struggled at times hoping that our decisions would be the right ones that would make our brother's transition into Heaven a peaceful one.

I let myself get so close to my brother which made it all the harder on myself when the time came to say goodbye. My sister commented by letting me know that I would still have done it the same way. I often wondered where I would be when it was time for him to go. Would I be sleeping, be in church praying, traveling, grocery shopping at Giant Eagle, or out buying another silly pair of shoes? Would I get to be there right beside him, or would he have to do it on his own?

Out of all the gifts that my brother has given me, he gave me the best gift possible. He let me be there to hold his hand and pray. Mike and I sat there and read some of the pages of my book to him. We sat patiently and listened to religious music. I watched his hospital gown go up and down and his deep abdominal breathing begin to become shallower. I found myself breathing right along with him, which at times was very fast and eventually slowed down. Amazing Grace was playing on the tv music station, which was so fitting because it was one of his favorite songs. It may sound all so dramatic, but there was a sense of calmness and pure peace in his room with me, my husband, Mike, and two of his private duty nurses, Debbie and Danette.

My husband went down to the cafeteria to get some coffee because it seemed like we had a little more time. A little monitor lay in my brother's lap which recorded his heart rate, respiration, and oxygen level. Even though my brother's numbers on the monitor were steady, I didn't take my eyes off him. I began to count the diamond, octagon and moon shapes on his hospital gown. We called family and friends to say their last goodbyes. Listening to their last words to him was not easy for me. Their voices tried to be strong, but you could hear the sadness and quivering in their voices. Suddenly, the numbers on the monitor began to plummet, going down one number every second. I was doing the count down in my head. The monitor also read, 'weak pulse.' I immediately wanted to call out to God and ask for one more day or one more hour with him. I almost wanted to shout out that I'd take even "Five More Minutes," like in the Scotty McCreery song. I decided not to because this wasn't about me, but it was all about my brother.

I called my husband to see where he was as he walked off the elevator next to my brother's room. Mike walked into the room and stood at the foot of the bed. I watched my brother take his last breath and watched his heart stop beating on the monitor. The numbers on the monitor now read zero! A picture of that monitor will be etched in my head forever. He was gone! He waited for Mike! Coffee and Mike were the two important staples in his life after God and he loved all three. Mike was the constant who helped my brother and me get through the last ten years. For that I am eternally grateful.

Father Steve's great nephew, Vinny gave him a Pete the Penguin stuffed animal. Pete the Penguin is the Youngstown State University mascot. I placed Pete up high by the tv and Father Steve said that him and Pete would have a starring contest. Unfortunately, Pete won because he came home with us, and Father Steve didn't. Pete was later placed in the casket along with pictures and art activities from Jacob, Vinny, Isabella, Caleb, Gianna and Alaina. Since my brother got impatient and couldn't wait for this book to be published, I placed a printout of my book with a card and bookmark for him to take with him to read at his leisure. A beautiful spray of yellow roses and sunflowers adorned his casket.

Father Steve passed away wearing a bracelet with the Bible verse on it from John 6:35. This bible verse reads: Jesus says to them, "I am the bread of life; whoever comes to me will never hunger, and whoever believes in me will never thirst." He was also holding a pair of rosary beads that were once used for prayer by Bob Cene, a great friend of his. The rosary beads were from Gethsemane. Bob passed away recently and I'm sure he was waiting at heaven's door for

Father Steve. I can't imagine the mischief that they'll get into while in Heaven.

An announcement of Father's Steve's passing made the front page of the Vindicator, our local newspaper. The picture on the page showed my brother celebrating Easter Mass at Windsor House in Liberty, Ohio on April 16, 2017.

My brother went out in style. He was a very humble man, so I'm sure as he watched from Heaven he would have been impressed, yet would say, "What's all the fuss about?" The turnout at the calling hours was overwhelming. So many people came to show their respect, shared a story or two about him, and reached out to our family for anything that they might want or need. It warmed my heart!

In the morning, we all said our goodbyes and slowly entered the limo. Snow was coming down like crazy and looked so beautiful. My sister, Liz and brother, John, waited and watched the funeral director put my brother's Chosen hat on his head. It was so fitting because he loved watching Jesus in the movie. He even wore it while he was in the hospital. What a way to end his life on earth! At that moment a yellow rose fell out of the flower spray that was on top of the casket as they closed it. Liz immediately brought it to me and those rose petals will be saved forever. He then had a police escort to the church.

Participants at Mass included close relatives. His pall bearers consisted of his best friends. This was so very fitting because they were six friends who helped carry him during his last ten years either at physical therapy, water therapy, or with prayer. A song titled, "He Ain't Heavy, He's My Brother" is a ballad written by Bobby Scott and Bob Rusell. The Hollies and Neil Diamond famously sang it. Those six friends carried him as if Father Steve was their brother, never just a friend! So many of you carried him too, maybe not physically, but through communication, prayer and continued support. You gave him and his family what they needed to make it through ten years of daily unpredictability. Thank you!

Most Reverend Bishop David J. Bonnar was the Presider at the Mass of Resurrection for Father Steve. Bishop Bonnar made sure that the Mass was beautiful and fitting for such a faith-filled priest. His fond and kind words about my brother and gentle voice made the service peaceful and calming from the greeting all the way to the Prayer of Commendation as Salve Regina was sung. It helped my family and me get through Mass a little easier. Many priests attended his service for the heartwarming send off. When they joined each other in song, it sounded like a choir fit for Heaven. Father Edward Noga was the Homilist at Mass who spoke so highly of Father Steve. His talk gave me goose bumps. It was a genuine talk about Father Steve, a priest, who loved being a priest. They were described as best friends who stuck together till the end. I'm not sure how he got through his talk. My brother gave my sister, Liz and I the strength and courage to speak words of remembrance about him, something I didn't think that we would be able to do. The Holy Spirit worked within us. I wore pink to celebrate the life of such a great human being and priest. The Mass ended with Bishop Bonnar giving everyone a blessing and adding some inspirational words about my brother. We walked out of church singing, "When the Saints Go Marching In." A tough chapel visit at the cemetery was next as friends and relatives prayed and said their last goodbyes. A beautiful luncheon reception followed with many in attendance to share stories, and fellowship.

It was now time for my family to head back home, many miles away from me. Saying goodbye was so tough. A little hug turned into a huge one. I became courageous and decided to visit the cemetery where my brother was buried, next to my parents, to pray and reflect. How do I face the fact that I will no longer get to spend time with the man who changed my life? I will have to rely on countless priceless memories. I do know that if I look up to the sky and see the blue sky appear to be shaking, I'll simply know that there is a lot of polka dancing going on up there with my brother and parents or could it possibly be his motorcycle?

As I approached my brother's final resting place, I noticed something unusual. The spray of flowers from the calling hours were placed on top the mound of soil at the cemetery. It has been exceptionally cold and freezing here in Ohio, so the flowers were wet and partially frozen from the snowfall. However, there were two roses on the top of the spray of flowers that caught my eye. He left a sign for Mike and me to let us know that he was okay. Two yellow roses on the top of the spray were pointing up to Heaven and they appeared as though someone had just placed them there, not wet or frozen at all. They looked as if they had just bloomed. Yes, Father Steve is okay!

It's now time for me to spend more time with my family and discover something new to fill the spare time that I will now have and try to fill the void in my heart.

I will always remember that God is good!

ABOUT THE AUTHOR

Margie Cretella resides in Austintown, Ohio, with her husband, Mike. She got her inspiration to write a book from a new friend, Barb, who encouraged her to enjoy the writing process and turn her words into a book to share with others. Thanks to Barb, she loved the experience.

Margie wrote the book because she felt that she owed it to God and to her brother. She felt that she needed to share with the world that, yes, God is indeed good and is right there holding your hand every day especially during a tragedy. Margie wanted to share the faith-filled life that her brother experiences never giving up on this good God.

Margie loves her faith and her church, Immaculate Heart of Mary, in Austintown, Ohio. She especially loves being a Eucharistic minister, distributing the body and blood of Christ and volunteering at their food pantry serving about three hundred families.

She loves spending quality time with her husband, siblings, and spending time down south with her sons, daughters-in-law and grandchildren. Her son, Mikey, wife, Risa and grandson, Vinny have included Margie and Mike on some of their vacations. Margie and Mike love visiting their home in Clover, South Carolina, and swimming in their pool with Vinny. Margie and Mike love going for a boat ride with Mikey, Risa, and Vinny on Lake Wylie. They also have fun when they all get a bite to eat at Papa Doc's, their favorite waterfront restaurant. Many special times are spent in Charleston, South Carolina, with her son, Tony, his wife, Stefanie, and Margie's grandchildren, Bella and Caleb. They love going to Shem Creek to watch the dolphins and dine at a waterfront restaurant. They in turn love their visits to Ohio during the Christmas season eagerly waiting for snow to play in since they don't get any back home. A trip to Georgia is always enjoyed when Margie and Mike go to visit their son, Joe, his wife, Rachel, and Margie's grandchildren, Giana and Alaina. Their favorite times are visiting the Cathedral Basilica of St. John the Baptist in Savannah where they all light candles for the whole family. Joe's family has a big picnic, maybe some fishing and lightning up the sky on the Fourth of July, another wonderful time.

Margie loves Christmas and begins decorating the day after Halloween and leaving everything up until Valentine's Day. Her husband has given up on trying to reason with her and just lets her go because "that's her thing." Plus, she won't give up the Hallmark and Lifetime Christmas movies.

She loves taking care of her plants inside and gardening outside. She loves a beautiful, wintry, snowy day. She's like a little kid waiting for the very first snowfall of the season. If she stays inside, she'll be busy at her sewing machine.

Margie is a big fan of country music and attended the Country Music Fest in Nashville several times with Mike.

Much of her time is spent with Father Steve where every visit is a blessed adventure!